W9-ARQ-699

Words of Praise for Ken Tanner's *Never Order Barbecue in Maine*

"I love this book! Short on the usual lectures and tall on practical, tried-and-true coaching tips for achieving the competitive edge at work, it's a book every new grad (and even some old ones) should read."

Lois P. Frankel, Ph.D., Los Angeles, CA— Host of Eye on Your Career
and author of *Nice Girls Don't Get the Corner Office*.

"I know too many people who are frustrated with their workplace. If only they had read *Never Order Barbecue in Maine*! But it's never too late . . . I am going to present a copy of this book to my dearest friends."

Anand Chhatpar, Madison, WI—CEO, BrainReactions LLC
Named by *BusinessWeek* as "One of the Best Entrepreneurs Under 25"

"Whoever says there's nothing new under the sun hasn't yet read *Never Order Barbecue in Maine*. Proven career strategies? Ken's real-world advice is right on target. From building your image to managing your boss to finding new opportunities, the advice in this book is ethical, practical, and solid. Read this book and watch your career take off!"

Dick Bott, Overland Park, KS—CEO, Bott Radio Network

"The chapter on playing office politics with integrity is worth the price of this book all by itself. But you get so much more—like fueling your career by figuring out what you do best, how to recover from setbacks, and what it really takes to get that dream job. (Just ask Jay Leno.)"

Stone Peyton, Atlanta, GA—Author, leadership trainer and motivational speaker

"I studied Ken's real-world advice when trying to land a must-have job. When my car broke down on the way to a critical interview, I recalled his advice on turning negatives into positives—and he had used this exact possibility as an example. So, instead of panicking, I used the event to show them how well I can handle pressure. I got the job!"

Michelle Moberg, Eden Prairie, MN

"Ken shows how to build a career without sacrificing your integrity in the process. With so many others suggesting it's OK step on your coworkers to get ahead, that's a breath of fresh air. At the same time, Ken's strategies aren't of the 'goody two shoes' variety. His is real-world advice that's both practical and effective."

Greg Black, Atlanta, GA—National radio news anchor

NEVER ORDER BARBECUE IN MAINE

Proven Career Strategies
from People Who've Been There, Done That

KEN TANNER

NELSON BUSINESS
A Division of Thomas Nelson Publishers
Since 1798

www.thomasnelson.com

For Mom

Blanche Baggett Tanner who, along with the other women of our greatest generation, preserved this country during its great crises, faced life with dignity and wisdom, and prayed God's blessings upon her family and neighbors.

Stories are used throughout this book to illustrate the principles and strategies being discussed. Many of these stories are reproduced exactly as they occurred or even in the participants' exact words. These can be identified by the use of the individual's full name. Some people allowed me to use their stories but asked that their names not be used for privacy reasons. I substituted a fictitious first name in these cases. Most stories are based on actual events and molded to better fit the point being made. These can also be identified by the use of a first name only.

Several stories are pure fiction and—as they say in the movies—any resemblance to any person, living or dead, is purely coincidental. Any references to Cousin Ralph or any such family member obviously fit into this category. Also, every story in the chapter "Listen to Your Mom" is fiction and does not refer to any actual person or event.

Published in Nashville, Tennessee, by Thomas Nelson, Inc.

Nelson Book titles may be purchased in bulk for educational, business, fund-raising, or sales promotional use. For information, please e-mail: SpecialMarkets@ThomasNelson.com.

Scripture quotations are from The Holy Bible, KING JAMES VERSION.

Library of Congress Cataloging-in-Publication Data

Tanner, Ken.

Never order barbecue in Maine : proven career strategies from people who've been there, done that / Ken Tanner.

p. cm.

ISBN 0-7852-1349-X (hardcover)

1. Career development. I. Title.

HF5381.T234 2006

650.14--dc22

2005035062

Printed in the United States of America

06 07 08 09 10 QW 9 8 7 6 5 4 3 2 1

CONTENTS

Section III
REFINE YOUR CAREER

PREFACE

I WAS JUST OUT OF HIGH SCHOOL WHEN I RECEIVED AN invitation to attend a program in Chicago sponsored by the American Academy of Achievement. This organization held a yearly event in which it brought together one hundred "Young Leaders of Tomorrow" with thirty famous people. For a week I rubbed elbows with Neil Armstrong, Howard Baker, Michael DeBakey, and Sir Edmund Hillary (who responded to my question rather indignantly: "Why did I climb Mount Everest? Because, hell, boy, I like to climb mountains. You're thinking of the chap that climbed the Matterhorn."). And we listened to inspirational speeches from people like Lowell Thomas (who said everyone should go to jail at least once) and Dr. Jim Jenson, who had recently discovered the world's largest dinosaur. (His pearl: "No one would have paid any attention to me if I had discovered the world's smallest dinosaur.")

Most of the advice and thoughts I heard during this week were not as cleverly phrased; however, I harvested an abundance of plainspoken wisdom derived from years of experience. The president of General Motors—the employer of 700,000 people—chatted about dealing with people on an individual basis. A now-paralyzed Olympic champion taught us how she hurdles *real* obstacles these days. And, as detailed later in this book, a young executive provided surprising insight about how he used relationships to become president of a major corporation when he was barely out of his twenties. This week was the best educational experience of my life. Nothing compared to sitting at the feet of great men and women while they reminisced of their successes, failures, and dreams yet to be realized.

How different this seems when you survey the offering of problem-solving advice in business books and magazines, and from consultants and other so-called gurus. While there is some comfort in confident advice from MBAs, media stars, and gimmick-of-the-month programs, you often get the feeling that much of it is all frosting and no cake. Why? The latest theories and pontifications haven't been tested properly. Or those offering the advice are still wet behind the ears. Or a very successful person will assume that what brought him or her success will work for anyone else.

Whenever I am faced with a new problem, I tell myself, *Someone has faced this before. All I need to do is find out how that individual dealt with it successfully and duplicate the solution. I can skip the time-consuming analysis and risky weighing of possible options that others struggled with as they searched for solutions. I can use their pain to avoid some of the trial-and-error and skip right to the successful solutions.*

That's the idea of this book. We will examine career strategies from different angles. But each angle has one thing in common: it's based on the actual experiences of people who had some success in their careers—including me. These strategies are *proven* to work. You'll find chapters on building your career, developing relationships, avoiding career mishaps, coping with your job, and bouncing back from adversity. You'll learn how to market yourself, manage your boss, get promoted, and cope with stress. But all these chapters will be in service of one central idea: attaining a more satisfying career, whatever that means to you. (And we'll even help you sort out your thoughts there.)

Naturally, the book contains much of what I learned along the way. In fact, it contains just about all that I learned in the many jobs I've held over the past thirty years. Like the others in this book, I earned wisdom the hard way. My education in the school of hard knocks began in a Pizza Hut kitchen. It continued while eventually serving as regional operator, national training director, and vice president of a couple of international fast-food chains, interspersed with a two-year venture owning and operating a dinner theater and eventually jumping into the world of consulting. Even as a consultant I varied my expertise, first focusing on recruiting and now centering my practice on advising companies on better employee-retention practices. I've had the opportunity to look at careers and their development from below, from above, and from the sidelines. I've seen what does (and does not) work, I've studied the gurus, and I've laughed at the fads. And I've listened to a lot of smart people who shared incredible wisdom.

But let me emphasize that this is not *Ken Tanner's Formula for Success Book.* I have followed my own crooked path, stumbled into my own unique surprises, and tripped along my own journey into my personal definition of success. Both my journey and my destination probably vary dramatically from your experiences and what you are seeking. While this book features a lot of my opinions, anecdotes, clever uses of adverbs and adjectives, and, yes, advice, I ensure that you hear other views from men and women who have attained conventional definitions of success.

Perhaps the most enjoyable part of writing this book has come from interviewing dozens of successful people and asking each this same question: "What do you know now that you wish you had known then?" The answers were often surprising. Some included solid practical advice. Some waxed philosophical. Some folks responded with their tongues solidly planted in their cheeks. But all these people honored us with their insight.

Considering their achievements, their advice is well worth listening to.

You may notice conflicting advice in this book. As any great master will tell you, there are many routes to the top of the mountain. That's why you'll find alternatives to much of what I recommend—thanks to the many successful, generous people who offered nuggets of pure gold. And don't bother to try reconciling the different theories. Every person comes from a different starting point and has a different destination. Thus, your vehicle to the good life will be different from that of another reader's. Besides, the knowledge you need most will most likely reach out and grab you by the throat.

You will also notice that there is a lot of material *not* covered in this book. For instance, my discussion of résumés fails to teach you how to write a résumé. The discussion of interviewing does not include a listing of "great answers to interview questions." I did this because this ground has been covered ad nauseam. Just visit a bookstore and you will find the shelves covered with (often bad) books offering advice on résumés and interviewing. I chose not to replow this ground. Instead, I'll focus my comments on areas that have been overlooked or with which I disagree (and there are lots of these). As a result, very little of what's in this book is already on your bookshelf.

Comprehensive? Not possible. And you might find that to be a bit frustrating. Although I hope I have presented a heap of useful and productive advice, it is just not possible to address every career issue or to outline the one surefire path to glory. But within these pages you will find the major topics you need to explore in shaping your career and see some of the solutions to common issues that others have found. Use this for direction and reflection; save the details for your own unique journey—to the job or position in life that will provide the maximum amount of satisfaction.

Section I

DEFINE YOUR CAREER

1

FIND YOUR SWEET SPOT

DURING MY BRIEF RESIDENCE IN ALABAMA, I HAD THE opportunity to see Michael Jordan play right field for the Birmingham Barons, the AA farm team for the Chicago White Sox. Jordan's fame and charisma filled the ballpark that season. He was gracious with the fans, incredible with the kids, and completely respectful to his teammates. As a person, he was a credit to the game, the city, and himself. But as a baseball player, Michael Jordan was adequate at best. He was competent, but AA ballplayers must be much more than that if they ever expect to play in the big leagues. Jordan certainly gave it his best shot, but he never made a major-league roster. He just wasn't good enough.

Ponder that statement for a moment. *Michael Jordan just wasn't good enough.* He is perhaps the greatest basketball player who ever lived. An argument could be made that no one has ever dominated any sport to the extent Jordan dominated his. Yet despite his best efforts—and nobody tries harder than Michael Jordan—the best he could be in another sport was an "adequate" minor leaguer.

Billy Graham would have been a terrible plumber. Albert Einstein would have failed as a salesman. Donald Trump would make a poor accountant. Follow the wrong career path, and you, like Mike in baseball, will be doomed to mediocrity, struggle, and frustration.

When I coach people on career pursuit, I have them focus on discovering their real talent. Finding your talent is that important to your career. It is a natural conclusion, based on the fact that when I talk to people who are unhappy with—or even hate—their jobs, I can usually find a strong talent their career does not even use.

> Despite his best efforts—and nobody tries harder than Michael Jordan—the best he could be in another sport was an "adequate" minor leaguer.

In a perfect world, you would find your sweet spot just before entering college. Then you could study all the appropriate subjects, make all the "right" contacts, and enter your ideal job the day after graduation. But this is not how life really works, is it?

In fact, most people spend the first stage of their careers just searching for their niche. All the planning and personal reflection fall by the wayside when life erupts. Marriage, babies, mortgages, and all the many other things that make up life affect your choice of jobs and careers more than careful planning can sometimes overcome. Don't be discouraged if you are reading this at age thirty, forty, fifty, or beyond. The initiation of adulthood is not the only time in your life to search for your sweet spot.

Also realize that finding your signature in your career is not something that can only happen with a clean slate. Much of the reflection needed cannot be done without some life experiences to use as a reference. Think about this: Can you really trust the entirety of your career to a decision you made at age twenty?

Finding your sweet spot is rarely a one-time event. Your needs and desires will evolve; finding a satisfying career will probably do so as well. It is never too late to redirect your career to fit your real calling.

How Do You Find Your Talent?

Actually, your talent usually finds you at an early age. Talent doesn't change. In that sense, it is not like your skills and interests. If you have a particular talent as a teenager, you're probably going to have that talent throughout your life. You don't lose it. Your talent is always there (barring unforeseen tragedy), even if you neglect it or fail to exploit it.

Yet some people have talents they are not aware of. They excel at something but just assume everyone has the ability. I have a friend who is an excellent writer. He didn't know this until a report he wrote at work was returned with a note from his boss: "Outstanding! You write extremely well!" While he now acknowledges this ability and uses it in his work, he didn't realize his abilities until he accidentally found out.

I know of a young lady who seems to bond with children easily. Kids love her the minute they meet her. Yet she had to have this pointed out to her; she just assumed that was the way it was for everyone. She's now trying to combine her interest in art with this natural charisma she possesses. I predict that she will grow a remarkable career, one that combines her talent with her interests.

> Can you really trust the entirety of your career to a decision you made at age twenty?

One stop on the journey to discovering your sweet spot is discovering where your talents are *not.* A good way to recognize that you are playing the wrong game is when you have to work hard to achieve mediocre results. Now, it's OK to be average, just as long as you don't have to work hard to get there. If it takes little effort to just meet minimum standards, and if being mediocre is fine with you, no problem. But if you have to struggle to meet the minimum, then

Working hard to achieve greatness—that's OK. Working hard to keep your head above water—time to play a new game.

you are in the wrong game. If you are in the right line of work, you'll easily meet minimum standards, and extraordinary efforts will yield extraordinary results.

Working hard to achieve greatness—that's OK. Working hard to keep your head above water—time to play a new game.

Don't Order Barbecue in Maine

Our family has a fun vacation tradition. Our first night in a state, we dine on the local specialty. For instance, we'll eat crab cakes in Maryland; catfish in Mississippi; beef stew in Connecticut; and tree bark in California. While driving along the New England coast, we pulled into a seaside restaurant in Maine. You can guess what local delicacy was on our minds.

I was thrown off my game when the waitress informed me they had just run out of lobster. Not wanting fish, I instead ordered barbecue ribs. As we were finishing up our dinner, the waitress asked how I liked my entree. "Well," I replied, "ordering ribs in Maine was about as smart as ordering lobster in Memphis." Translation: barbecue is not among Maine's strengths. I should have gone with seafood. Always go for the strengths.

You should go with your strengths when choosing your career. Don't put a square peg in a round hole, don't order barbecue in Maine, and don't become a lawyer if your talent is sales.

Similarly, you should go with your strengths when choosing your career. Don't put a square peg in a round hole, don't order barbecue in Maine, and don't become a lawyer if your talent is sales. Does this mean that if you have the talent for drawing, you should be an artist? If you are an excellent athlete, you should focus on an NBA career? No. Do not limit your career selection to a field that uses *only* your talent. Instead, look at your talent as a direction for exploring many career directions. Good writers can indeed become authors. But they may also find satisfaction in public relations, copywriting, publishing, research, teaching, and a myriad of business situations. The point is to find a career that makes liberal *use* of your talent.

> Far and away the best prize that life offers is the chance to work hard at work worth doing.
>
> —Theodore Roosevelt

Know Thyself

It is important to know what you like, where you thrive, and the environment and culture that put you at your best. Taking vocational tests or engaging a formal analyst is often helpful, but you can do much of your analysis through personal reflection. Find a quiet moment and ask yourself some questions. Notice how the answers tend to overlap and form a pattern. It will put you well on your way to identifying where you want your career to be.

What Are Your Skills, Talents, and Special Knowledge?

Write down the things you know from education, training, hobbies, family experiences, and other sources. Identify the talents you possess; they often will directly lead you to your life's work. Look for patterns in this list. There is usually a reason that you selected a certain course of study or degree program. Your talents, interests, and hobbies frequently overlap. Don't be surprised if this list of education, talents, and skills points you to an easily identifiable career path.

What Types of People Do You Want to Work With?

Do you like to compete (which might lead you to a sales environment), or do you prefer a team approach (such as that found in the military or research)? Some people like being around a diverse workforce so they can constantly experience new ideas and cultures; others prefer the comfort of the familiar. Do you want to be exposed to creative people, hard chargers, intellectuals, athletes? Artists, accountants, lawyers, ministers? What types of people bring out the best in you and help you accomplish your goals?

What Type of Work Environment Do You Prefer?

Do you favor a casual-dress environment, or does putting on a suit make you feel more professional? Do you enjoy a social setting, or would you rather have a "strictly business" relationship with your coworkers? Do you prefer to work in a nice office with a skyline view, or does sitting in a forest tower appeal to you?

> Everyone must row with the oars he has.
>
> —English proverb

Actually, that *extreme* of a choice is easy to make; you should focus on more subtle variations. For instance, inside salespeople often work in an open environment where all the desks can be seen in one glance, while researchers are usually closeted in private settings with little distraction or interaction. To some, this distinction is of no significance. To others, it could mean the difference between thriving and going insane.

What Style of Organization Makes You Comfortable?

Do you like a small company where everyone knows one another and you have full access to top executives? Or do you prefer a large corporation with an unlimited career path? Do you prefer a management style where everyone seems to do a little bit of everything, or one with a clearly defined job description? How much interaction with clients or customers do you like?

How Much Time Do You Want to Put In?

I began my career working eighty-hour weeks and never saw a weekend off. My best friend worked for the government. Although I was making about three times what he was, he mentioned one day that he couldn't imagine working weekends or more than forty hours a week. At that time in my life, I couldn't fathom anything else.

What trade-offs will you make for money? How much time do you want to spend with your family? To what extent are you willing to let your career be a part of your life? These are all important considerations when deciding on a career path. Most jobs have a definite and identifiable time frame attached to them. Identify this factor early on in your decision-making process, because it will absolutely eliminate certain career paths.

Are You Willing to Travel? Relocate?

I had a boss who once held an incredible job. He was the officer who gave morning security briefings to the chief of naval operations. His career was on the fast track; he was destined to become an admiral. Instead, he chose to leave the navy and work in the private sector. Why? The next step in his career was to command a ship, and he just didn't want to be away from his family for more than a day at a time.

Some great jobs involve extensive travel. No such job will be satisfying if it conflicts with your perception of the right way to build a family. Likewise, some professions, such as management and the military, require frequent relocation. Don't even consider a profession like this if the thought of leaving your hometown is traumatic.

Likewise, consider potential relocation when evaluating a specific company. For instance, if your goal is to work into senior management with a specific company, the only way to do this is to eventually live where the company has its headquarters. You cannot reach the top with FedEx if you won't live in Memphis, with Microsoft if you don't like Seattle, or with Ford if Detroit is too cold for you.

> Neglect not the gift that is in thee.
>
> —1 Timothy 4:14

How Much Money Do You Want to Make?

You are grinning as you say, "Millions!" But this question really doesn't usually have such an obvious answer. Most people have a material goal they must achieve, a lifestyle that they want to reach, and they will do any job necessary to reach that point. For instance, you may want a four-bedroom house in the suburbs and enough money to go out for dinner once or twice a week. You work hard, and eventually you reach this goal.

Once you do, however, you may find yourself looking for things besides money or material items to satisfy you. And that's when the nature of the work becomes far more important than incremental income.

So, get a good handle on where money shakes out at different levels in your priorities. For instance, you might decide that you must make $40,000 to support the basic lifestyle your family needs. But after that, time off, vacations, and hobbies become more important. So, assuming other planets are aligned, you may choose to become a high school teacher. You'll likely be able to make the $40,000 (but not a whole lot more) and have summers off to pursue travel and other priorities.

What Is Important to You?

Do you have values you want to include in your career? For example, some people want to work to feed the hungry, gain power or prestige, or build landmarks that will stand for generations. Think about what is important to you and how you might incorporate this in your next job.

Dale Naftzger, an entrepreneur from Portland, Oregon, comments:

> Distinguish between monetary income and psychological income. Do not confuse money with happiness. On the other hand, do not confuse poverty with happiness either. Be honest, and guiltless, about what truly makes you happy. Pursue what brings you joy. Says Harlan Naftzger, my father, "Greatness is measured by the quality of your life, not the quality of your career."

Hot Vocations for the Future

Some people try to mold their future by picking the hot industries of the future. Predicting the top occupations of the future is like trying to time the stock market. There are just too many factors to take into consideration, too many variables in history, to come up with any accurate projection.

In fact, prognostications of future careers are about as accurate as those predicting future inventions. Remember all the descriptions of the future that were made when we were growing up? The cliché always began with, *"By the year 2000…"* The phrase was then followed with images of flying cars, three-hour workweeks, the end of all disease, and chemically enhanced baseball players routinely hitting fifty home runs. (OK, that one came true.)

> Where your talents and the world's needs cross, there lies your vocation.
>
> —Aristotle

Predicting hot career areas is pretty much like that. Such predictions tend to focus on wild and exotic possibilities, while the fact is that most jobs of the future will be quite similar to the jobs of today. Sure, cloning might yet become a big industry, but they'll still need good, old-fashioned lawyers, accountants, and salespeople to staff the companies. (As well as mechanics to work on all those flying cars!) My point is, don't get all twisted up worrying about how the future will change the job market.

> It is never too late to be what you might have been.
>
> —George Eliot

Let me break my rule here and function as a visionary guru. I am going to predict the hot jobs from now through 2020. Here they are:

- Teacher
- Nurse
- Accountant
- Sales rep
- Mechanic
- Engineer
- Lawyer
- Electrician
- Police officer
- Firefighter

Some new, sexy occupations just might be created in the next couple of decades, but I can *guarantee* that these jobs will be solid opportunities for the future. There are two reasons. First, these professions are basic and always needed. Society will always require teachers, emergency workers, and contractors. Maybe the nature of the professions will change, but the career fields will always be there.

But the biggest reason for this job security is that these critical positions are currently being held by baby boomers. Remember, jobs don't just come open when new industries are created. They also become available when existing workers move to other occupations or retire. The baby boomers began retiring in 2006. Boomers make up a disproportionate segment of the population, and positions will be vacated as they retire. Generation Xers are a significantly smaller group than the boomers. This will create a serious talent shortage over the next two decades. In fact, the Bureau of Labor Statistics projects that through 2010, the number of job openings resulting from replacement needs is greater than that of openings resulting from employment growth.

Troy Wough, president of The Rainmaker Academy of Nashville, recounts this story:

> I had dinner with several partners at an accounting firm the evening before conducting a sales-training program at their accounting firm. I knew this would be a good time to pick up some information that would help me the next day. Earlier I had learned that they had niches in health care, auto dealers, construction, manufacturing, wholesalers, community banking, and not-for-profits. It seemed to me to be a lot of niches for a small firm. Alarm bells went off.
>
> My assessment was confirmed when I asked the partner leading the health-care niche, "How many physicians in your city?" Her puzzled expression was the look I often get when I ask a niche specialist the size of the prospect base. Here is a fact about companies: *Having many niches means having no niches at all.*
>
> This same principle applies to people, and I found that out early in my own career. I was way too diffused, too much of a dabbler. Now, I know that you are most likely to have success when you focus on one field. Learn the details of

> We've all been blessed with God-given talents. Mine just happens to be beatin' up people.
>
> —Sugar Ray Leonard

> the job, the recurring problems of the industry, and the subtle nuances that often separate success from failure. When you specialize, you learn how to read the customer base and develop a sixth sense for anticipating emergencies and opportunities.
>
> I tell my clients (and I focus completely on CPA firms, by the way) that to have a profitable, enjoyable practice, you must offer superior skills to a clearly identified niche. Your clients must know that you are a specialist with expert skills in their areas. Niche specialization is the key to future success for CPA firms, as well as for people building their personal careers.

In my research on this subject, I heard this same advice again and again. Focus on one dream. Specialize. Offer a service in which you are an expert and in which you will excel.

The Merger of Talent and Passion

Growing up as a boy in Alabama, my cousin Ralph struggled to determine his career direction. While working alongside his father in the family taxidermy business, he also went to veterinarian school at night. Ralph eventually found his calling by combining the two vocations. In fact, he opened a joint veterinary clinic and taxidermy shop. His slogan was a stroke of marketing genius: *Either way, you get your dog back.*

Here is a great example of merging talent and passion. Listen to this story from Blanche Pope Tosh, a teacher, actor, and author from Memphis, Tennessee.

> When people hear I taught high school speech and drama, I invariably get the same question: did you teach anybody famous? Their curiosity is satisfied when I list several successful actors, including

the star of a long-running children's television program, a Broadway actor, even an Academy Award winner. That seems to end the conversation for them, but for me the answer is so very incomplete.

So how do *I* evaluate my career? I don't think of the "stars"—though I am so proud of them. No, I think of the thousands of students I touched in different ways. The shy teenage girl who developed self-confidence by speaking in front of groups. The withdrawn young boy who began believing in himself by acting in a play. The countless students who trusted me with their problems and thoughts and allowed me to share my faith and beliefs with them.

Even today, I will hear from former students who credit me with their first jolt of self-confidence, or discovering the excitement of the spotlight, or the first time they were simply shown respect. They tell me of learning responsibility by being a stage manager, or organization from writing a speech, or how to think quickly on their feet by participating in a debate. Some of my students—who have now achieved dramatic successes in the world—tell me that their prize possession is a small, rusting trophy they won in a speech tournament many years ago.

It is good to be able to say you had a hand in some famous celebrity's career. But for me, it is so much more rewarding to know I've touched several thousand people in small, but quite significant, ways. I believe God puts situations in our paths. I took my talent, got involved in a career in which I'd cross many people's paths, and let God do the rest. It worked out pretty well for me.

Most people are not as lucky as Ralph and Blanche. They struggle for years—even their entire careers—looking for that beautiful alignment among talent, interest, and occupation. When a person finds that duplication, it is a powerful and satisfying merger.

2

BUILD YOUR PRODUCT—YOU

CONSIDER THE HUMBLE HERSHEY BAR. IT IS UNUSUAL among its candy bar competitors in that it is not a combination of anything. It is just a hunk of milk chocolate—outstanding milk chocolate for sure, but just a hunk of milk chocolate nonetheless. No peanuts, no nougat, no caramel. Just chocolate. Even without doing any advertising until 1970, the Hershey bar has been a best-selling product for more than a century.

So, what's my point? The last chapter implores you to find your talent and base your career on that talent. Good advice, but I may have misled you if you finished that chapter thinking that was the end of your journey to a great career. While there are cases of people who have flourished on talent alone (I can't think of any but will leave open the possibility), the Hershey-bar people are rare indeed. Everyone else must build on that raw talent, embellish it, and even advertise it aggressively in order to sell the product and have a satisfying career. I call that process *building your product*.

Building your product is a lifelong process. It includes your formal education, but it is individualized and enhanced by the many things you choose to teach yourself and learn on your own. Your education and development are continuously refined through the things you do to make yourself a better employee.

Develop Your Business Abilities

Although we usually think of formal education as the career building blocks, employers actually look for less-formal skills when seeking an employee. According to the U.S. Department of Labor, these are the skills that companies most want to see:

The Ability to Solve Problems

This is really the crux of it, isn't it? Yet this trait goes right over most people's heads. How many times have you heard someone say, "I could have gotten it done, but a problem got in the way"? People who build great careers understand that the only reason anyone is ever hired is to solve problems. If you have the ability and the attitude to solve problems, employers and promotions will beat a path to your door.

The Ability to Deal with People

This ability is not reserved for management. "Can't we all just get along?" could be the permanent cry of HR directors everywhere. On one level, the ability to deal with people refers to basic human relations: the ability of a person to function in society, work alongside diverse coworkers, and collaborate successfully with other employees. You must be able to blend into the team no matter where you work or what your level of responsibility.

> People who build great careers understand that the only reason anyone is ever hired is to solve problems.

On a broader level, the ability to create and grow this spirit in a leadership role will propel your career far ahead of your peers. All companies face inevitable problems dealing with how people interact with one another. The success of a company depends upon how well people can work together. Your ability to foster this society can make your whole career.

The Ability to Teach/Train

Training departments are usually the first victims of tight budgets. Yet workers still need to be trained and developed. This underscores the value of any worker to teach and train others. It not only applies to managers—who must do the bulk of training—but it also applies to the peer leader, helping the guy in the next cubicle to understand how a new spreadsheet operates. This ability is noted by the company and will enhance your career measurably.

The Ability to Communicate

People who communicate effectively will move ahead. People who communicate poorly will never approach their potential. Successful people must be able to express their opinions with logic and with influence. You must be able to write a succinct memo and a solid business letter, hold an intelligent conversation, and make a convincing business presentation.

The Ability to Demonstrate Basic Liberal Arts Skills

Do not overlook critical educational building blocks. Employers thirst for people who are solidly educated in math, science, and foreign languages. Once an absolute cornerstone of our education system, these critical skills have been pushed aside to allow more time for building self-esteem and understanding creative anthropology.

Colleges now require only the most basic courses, giving you substantial competitive advantage if you take advanced courses in math, science, and language. Imagine your increased value to an international wholesaler if you can speak fluent Spanish or

French. No matter what department you are climbing through, you will have a tremendous advantage over any competitor for the next job if you can communicate with the customer.

Develop Your Business Traits

Much of what determines a great career is not just what you know, but how you approach your work and even your life. Here are some qualities you can develop that will serve you well in your career.

Be a Peer Leader

It was 1982, and the Atlanta Braves were returning from the last game of the regular season. The players were tensely awaiting the result of the Dodgers / Giants game. If the Dodgers won, the Braves would be tied with them and have a one-game playoff. But if the Giants won, Atlanta would be outright champions of the National League Western Division.

About an hour into the flight, word came that the Giants had prevailed and the Braves had won the division by the slimmest of margins: one single game.

Amid the celebration sat Dale Murphy, National League MVP for two consecutive years. Not only was he the best player on the team, but he was probably the best player in baseball at the time. If anyone deserved the credit for the championship, it was Dale Murphy, which made the next thing he did that much more remarkable.

Murphy quietly went from seat to seat and had brief conversations with each team member. "Hey, Brett," he would say. "Do you remember that catch you made that saved two runs and let us win the Expos game? That's the game we won the division by." Then he'd move over and say to Bob, "Remember the home run you hit to beat the Mets in April? That's the game we won the division by." And he continued this, speaking with each player—star and benchwarmer alike—reminding him of one thing he did that allowed the team to win one game during the season. And that was always the one game that won the division championship.

> The as-if principle:
> If you want a quality,
> act as if you
> already have it.
>
> —William James

Dale Murphy didn't own the team, and he was not a manager. Nope, he was someone far more important. He was a peer leader.

Many people misunderstand the difference between management and leadership. While management is a formal, structural arrangement, leadership is a trait that can be exhibited by anyone in the organization. You do not need to have an impressive title or long tenure to be a peer leader. Demonstrate peer leadership within your group and you will see your value in the organization soar, your promotions will flow more quickly, and your work will be far more satisfying.

Be a Solution Finder

The advice to be a solution finder may appear to be another way of saying you need problem-solving skills, but I'm making a different point. The ability to solve problems is a skill; being a solution finder is more of an attitude. We all know people who declare that they are devil's advocates, challenging the system for its own good. In reality, they are pains in the rear. Anyone can find fault; anyone can uncover fault; anyone can tear down ideas. These actions are easy, require no talent, and create a cancer in the organization. An organization really cherishes someone who has the *mind-set* to find solutions. These are not Pollyannas, who are blind to problems. These are people who recognize that if not for problems, no one would have a job. Their attitude is: *Every problem has a solution.*

Develop Resilience

Stuff happens. Bad things really do happen to good people. Be able to cope with unfair comments, derailed suggestions, and business crises. Those around you observe how you react to setbacks. Learn to deal with bad things. People will notice who stays calm in battle and who keeps his head when others are losing theirs. Pick yourself up and move on.

Handle Conflict Appropriately

Some conflict will occur whenever strong personalities are gathered on a team. In fact, if two people agree on everything, one of them isn't necessary.

Conflict is inevitable, but combat is optional. Show your leadership by demonstrating your ability to disagree and be disagreed with. Become a model for healthy conflict, and the people responsible for your next promotion will note the contrast to most of your coworkers.

Develop a Positive Attitude

Dallas resident Bill Spae has been president of several well-known corporations. He shares his perspective of the most important personal trait that you can develop:

> You've *got* to have a great attitude. Good attitudes succeed; bad attitudes fail. It is as simple as that.
>
> People with great attitudes know the direction they want to go and pursue it with enthusiasm. When they run into a wall, their attitude will carry them in a new direction until they achieve their success.

You cannot achieve success without the support and participation of other people. But people will avoid—even shun—those with bad attitudes. You will fail because the very people you need will ignore you. On the other hand, people are attracted to enthusiastic folks with a bright attitude and enthusiasm. People will surround, support, and champion those who choose to stand in the sunlight.

Realize that attitude is an absolute choice, a personal decision. It is 100 percent controllable. No one can give it to you, and no one can take it from you. You are the beneficiary—or victim—of your own actions. This is completely in your own hands.

Other paths to success (such as advanced education, family connections, or superior talent) require an investment. This "cost" might include years of study, or powerful friends, or backbreaking work, or a lucky gene pool. These things can often be expensive, take a long time to cultivate, and even longer to see results. Not so with attitude. A positive, enthusiastic attitude doesn't require anyone else's contribution. Having a great attitude is immediate, it requires no education, and it is absolutely free.

Reject Perfection

I enjoy working around the house and was installing wood flooring in my library. I stood back, shook my head, and let out a disgusted sigh. My wife asked me what was the matter. "Look at that corner." I pointed to an area by a bookcase in which the boards were off by a quarter of an inch. "Our friends will notice that catastrophe," I analyzed.

"Listen to me," she said firmly. "Anybody who would notice that is just not someone we would want as a friend."

As impressive as it sounds, perfectionism is not a positive trait. Perfectionism is the need to see a project to the point at which it has no flaws, no errors, and everything exactly right. Since nothing ever meets this standard, the perfectionist is always in a state of disappointment and frustration. He drives subordinates crazy, and they feel completely unappreciated. The perfectionist's boss is also frustrated; projects are usually late and contain many unnecessary complications. Perfectionism leads to low self-esteem, difficulty working with peers, poor management abilities, and low productivity.

Perfectionists must learn to view the world, other people, themselves, and their work through different standards. Nothing is "perfect" if it is never completed. Learn to strike the proper balance between acceptable standards, promptness, and productivity.

Adopt an acceptable quality standard. Here's the best definition of *quality* I've ever heard: fitness for use. Anything beyond fitness for use is wasted time and money; anything less is also time and money lost. Determine the desired end result of each project, and target that standard. Rather than focusing on doing everything perfectly, think about all the stuff you'll be able to get to now.

Build Upon Your Strengths

Ted is an exceptional salesman. He can walk into an office and leave an hour later with a contract. No one is his peer when it comes to selling.

Ted should be working for a company and be the greatest salesman in its history. Instead, he opened his own company and manages a staff of salespeople. And that's a problem, because he has no management abilities whatsoever. He is disorganized, he is unable to motivate his staff, and he has no comprehension of what it takes to be a business owner.

The cruel joke is that Ted—like most people—completely

misunderstands his strengths and weaknesses. He actually believes that he is a good manager and makes no effort to acknowledge his shortcomings. But more important, he takes his true talent for granted. Because selling comes so naturally to him, Ted assumes it is easy for everyone. So he stays in the office, mismanaging his business, while mediocre salespeople are left on their own to hawk his products. Absolutely no one in the organization is working from strengths.

About once a year, you are called into your boss's office for your annual review. Here he will talk about the things you accomplished and how you rate with the objectives given for your job. He will go over your strengths in glowing terms and then discuss your weaknesses. He will analyze them to an agonizing degree and then set up a program to help you correct them.

Focus on exploiting your strengths, not fixing your weaknesses.

This is the wrong way to approach your development; convince your boss to take a different tack. Work together to produce a plan that focuses on exploiting your strengths, not fixing your weaknesses.

The fact is that no matter how much effort I apply, I will never be a decent golfer. I could buy the best clubs and have Tiger Woods himself give me lessons. The best possible outcome is that my score would improve from 277 to the mid-200s. However, if I placed that same effort in the service of one of my strengths or talents, I could perhaps move a small mountain. And so could you.

While you should certainly correct any job-critical deficiencies, do not focus on them for your career development. Bring your weaknesses up to a level that meets minimum standards; then focus your energies on increasing your abilities in areas in which you are particularly talented. That formula will best develop you as someone who is known for being able to deliver extraordinary results in some clearly definable areas. And that's rocket fuel for a career.

> Never feel the want of business. The man who qualifies himself well for his calling never fails of employment.
>
> —Thomas Jefferson

On the other hand . . . you should certainly *focus* on your strengths when building your product, but that does not mean you should *ignore* your weaknesses. Earlier I mentioned you should bring "job-critical" weaknesses up to an acceptable level. When you do so, you may discover some potential strengths just waiting to be noticed. Jeff Olson of Middleboro, Vermont, offers this perspective:

> I was afraid of public speaking and bad at it as a result. Instead of running from opportunities to speak in public, I spent four years in Toastmasters and became a pretty good speaker. Yes, I had it in me, but you couldn't have convinced me of that when I started.

Do not interpret my advice to develop your strengths as a license to ignore potential talents. There may be several magnificent abilities you have suppressed. Take the challenge to nurture your latent gifts. You may find a powerful tool for your career growth.

Pick the Right Company

Let's face it. Immediate situations usually govern job selection. Most people pick a company based on what is available at the time in the location they want to live.

But sometimes we do have opportunities to find that "perfect" work situation. For instance, we have time to do some research as we approach college graduation. We are sometimes forced to take a long-range view when we are laid off from a job or simply contemplating a midcareer change. Or some people have the incredible foresight to look for their next job while things are going well in their present job (the ideal). Let's look at some aspects in choosing a company.

Even a Mediocre Jockey Can Win a Race if He Rides a Good Horse

The most unfair statistic in baseball is a pitcher's win-loss record. If a pitcher gives up eleven runs but his team scores twelve, he gets credit for a win. However, if he holds the other team to just one run, but his team fails to score any, he gets a loss. The biggest factor affecting a pitcher's win-loss record is not his performance but that of his teammates. Pitchers on good teams have better win-loss records than pitchers on lousy ones.

Your career can work that way too. Good performances yield stellar results when you are employed by a company with the assets and talent to consistently succeed. But even the most brilliant businessperson will stumble when matched with a mediocre company that has trouble finding its way.

Seek out quality companies as you would seek out profitable stock purchases. Your performance will be magnified. You will be associating with other winners, and you will have many more opportunities for growth.

Work for a Boss on the Fast Track

Seeking out bosses who are clearly on the fast track has the same effect as working for a good company. Their reputations will attach themselves to you, they will take you with them as they rise, and you'll often be their obvious replacement when they climb to stellar heights.

Seek a Diverse Workplace

Even if you are not a minority, it makes sense to seek out a company that has credible diversity policies. Good diversity practices are an indication that the company is advanced in its thinking and puts serious planning into its hiring and promotion policies. *This advanced thinking will not be used exclusively for diversity policies.* A good diversity policy usually reflects a company's full slate of quality human resource policies in areas like training, employee development, evaluation, and succession planning.

Match Your Career Stage with the Company

Your needs change throughout your career. Your company selection can be heavily based on those needs. Consider these situations:

Early career: seek a name brand. Pick up your pedigree at the beginning of your career. Sure, you can learn a lot at Bob's Advertising Agency, but if you want to build your résumé, you would be better served to get General Mills, GE, or PepsiCo on your résumé.

Little fish, big pond. At the entry level, get exposure to the big picture and learn the craft well. You can do this best as a small part of a large organization. Observe how the specialists work and interact. Put yourself in the position of being able to transfer between many departments and tasks, exposing yourself to many diverse ways of doing things.

Midcareer: big fish, little pond. In midcareer, this is a way to build your name and enhance your industry reputation. You can build your résumé by having bigger titles and by having more responsibility in the big picture. This step comes right before big fish, big pond.

Big money, quick promotion. You may face a time in your career during which the formulas don't seem to work. An extraordinary peer group may be blocking your next step, your company may not be growing, or your industry may be in decline. Whatever the root cause, the tried-and-true methods are just not effective. Take big, calculated risks when your career seems stagnant. Sign on with a failing company or department or one experiencing an evident crisis. Seasoned executives will be bailing, conservative candidates will not apply, and the candidate pool for these high-paying/influential positions will be slight.

> Don't learn the tricks of the trade. Learn the trade.
>
> —Anonymous

Realize that there is enormous risk in this strategy, but if you can produce results, you will be able to catapult past your contemporaries in pay and prestige. Make your successes public, and you can come out of this situation with a stellar experience. Your reputation will grow, and you will have made incredible contacts.

When looking for security. There may be times in your career when you desire stability. You are tired of facing reorganizations, downsizings, and rightsizings. When looking for job security, adopt a career strategy that will lower your vulnerability to your job being eliminated.

Here are two strategies for stability. First, get involved directly in producing the product your company sells. Layoffs usually focus on support staff, leaving primary production barely affected. But suppose your career is in support? What if you are a marketing manager or an accountant? Then work for a company in which that trade is its actual product. For example, if you are an accountant, work for an accounting firm. If you're in marketing, work for a marketing firm, not the marketing department of a company.

Another strategy applies to those who are not in a specific profession. If you are in general management or supervision, for example, transfer to the department having most direct contact with the customer. Companies that are reorganizing tend to slice more positions the farther they are away from actual customer contact. Sales and operational positions carry the most stability because they directly create revenue. The closer you are to the revenue stream, and the farther you are from the expense ledger, the safer you are from downsizing.

Know Your End Game

Many people put as much thought into planning their careers as they do in selecting a place to eat lunch. The fact is, many careers progress by serendipity.

Opportunities present themselves at various stages of life; jobs pop up that meet immediate needs. For instance, many people go to work for a company because it was the first one that offered them a job right after they were laid off by their previous company. I am not being critical here, just identifying reality. Sometimes we make brilliant career plans—and then life happens; we must adjust.

This type of serendipitous career planning can, by itself, lead to fine career results. Take the case of Bruce, who is now the senior vice president for production for an international food company. In this highly responsible position, he oversees several hundred employees and a $200 million budget. It is the peak point of a magnificent career. Yet do you think that as a young lad of ten,

Bruce dreamed of someday being in charge of killing Croatian chickens for the world's third-largest agricultural company? Of course not. Bruce's destination job was the result of merging his talents with his education with his opportunities, all tempered by things that popped up during his life.

Careers just can't be planned in minute detail, nor should they be. Too much detailed planning may actually result in bigger disasters than no planning at all. If you plan too narrowly, you will miss opportunities as well as be a dinosaur in a changing world. Opportunities will present themselves that you never could have dreamed of when you began your career; the world will change in ways you never could have imagined as a child.

But let's find that sensible middle ground. Let me use Andre as an example here. I've recently become acquainted with this impressive young man and observed his process for making a job change. Andre was an emergency communications officer with the 911 system in Gwinnett County, Georgia, a suburb of Atlanta. He made the decision that his next job was to be a police officer. There are about a dozen quality police departments in the Atlanta area, but the opportunity with Gwinnett County was an obvious choice for him. He was already working for this county, so he was well involved in its pension plan and had accumulated many benefits. His work at the 911 center made him completely familiar with the county's procedures and policies. He had made good contacts within the department, and he knew the geography thoroughly. And besides, Gwinnett County paid better than any other force in the metro area. If Andre wanted to have a great career as a

> Many people put as much thought into planning their careers as they do in selecting a place to eat lunch.

police officer, it was clear that Gwinnett County offered him tremendous opportunity.

Instead, he chose to accept a position with Fulton County. This department did not offer as much money, and he had to start from scratch getting to know the system and the people in it. For a career as a police officer, this county could not offer the solid opportunity that Andre had in his own backyard. So why did he make this choice? He did it because being a police officer was not his end game.

> As a man thinketh in his heart, so is he.
>
> —King Solomon

Andre's career destination is to be in a senior position with the FBI, ATF, or DEA. To get there, Andre figures, he needs lots of experience with a variety of criminal situations. He would not get this with Gwinnett County, a place filled with upper-middle-class suburbs, where he'd be enforcing traffic laws and investigating noise violations instead of felonies.

Fulton County is a different story. Much of inner-city Atlanta is in this county, as well as many headquarters of international businesses. It also contains people of virtually every nationality and ethnic background. Fulton officers deal with a great deal of street crime, drug enforcement, and white-collar fraud cases.

While Gwinnett County offered a much better career as a *police officer,* Fulton presented Andre with the experience he needed to prepare for the FBI. He played the end game rather than looking at the immediate opportunity. That type of planning builds great careers. It seeks out opportunities for the destination position while fully acknowledging the opportunities that pop up in life.

Get an MBA—Maybe

You probably already have a college degree of some sort, so let's focus on one question: Should you get your MBA? Realize that securing higher education will not guarantee you anything. While it is true that, over the long haul, an MBA will pay off, you cannot rely on it as a quick fix for an otherwise lackluster career. It is better to look upon an MBA as a key. The more keys you have, the more doors you can unlock. So—to carry the analogy to ridiculous levels—the more doors will be open to you.

The MBA offers more to you than just credentials. First of all, what you learn in the program is actually applicable to real life. This is an astounding benefit not typically found within the walls of a university. You will find that case studies reviewed in class pop up in your work. Problems discussed in class rear their heads in the workplace, and you will have already talked through some potential solutions. Study groups often break out into discussions of actual scenarios that students are facing in the workplace, so you end up with your own little board of directors while taking courses.

> If you don't know where you are going, you might wind up someplace else.
>
> —Yogi Berra

Another huge benefit of graduate school is the tremendous network you build. You will get to know dozens of up-and-coming executives for all industries, who will cross your path many times throughout your career. Much like a fraternity, MBA students often form lifelong bonds.

Pursuing an MBA requires a serious sacrifice. It costs a lot of money. And you must invest significant time. But money is the easier hurdle to overcome. Student loans are simple to get and may not even be necessary if your company foots the bill (as most major corporations will do). If not, check with the financial aid officers for the school you will be attending; they can talk you through a myriad of options.

Time is your bigger investment. Determine whether you can afford to divert your attention from your present job. It would be tragic to lose your job because of poor performance caused by the demands your studies placed on your time.

Beyond Schooling: Watch Movies

You can spend fifty thousand dollars and two years of your life and earn an MBA. Or you can pop a tub of popcorn in the microwave and plop in front of your TV and learn all the business lessons you really need by watching classic old movies. You won't get to put any extra letters after your name, but the lessons you learn from cinema are usually more enduring and applicable than any lecture on macroeconomics.

Indirect learning can be more meaningful (and fun) than what happens in the classroom. Most people reading this probably grew up watching television, be it *Captain Kangaroo* or *Sesame Street*. This entertainment/learning can continue your whole life. Just look a couple of layers beneath the obvious. Your career will soar if you learn the lessons these movies provide:

Babe: Manage with influence rather than dominance.

Beauty and the Beast: Judge people by the character they demonstrate rather than first impressions.

Big Fish: What may look like a wild dream to you just might be solid reality to someone else.

Braveheart: Watch how a leader inspires.

Chariots of Fire: No matter what the obstacles, you can accomplish the mission.

A Face in the Crowd: Hypocrisy will eventually find a way to catch up with you.

Hoosiers: This movie illustrates so many leadership traits and team-building basics that it can be accused of being an industrial training film with a basketball subplot.

It's a Wonderful Life: Put your problems in perspective.

A League of Their Own: As Ann Richards once said, "Ginger Rogers did everything Fred Astaire did, only backwards and in high heels." All questions about women's equality and ability to function in the workplace should have come to an end during World War II, when women ran this country while men were fighting the war.

Miracle on 34th Street: At least once in your career, go ahead and fight for a hopeless cause.

Mr. Smith Goes to Washington: Truth will win out in the end if honest men refuse to be beaten.

Saving Private Ryan: Courage is not an absence of fear; it is doing the job despite your terror.

Schindler's List: One man—even a terribly flawed one—*can* make a difference.

The Third Man: We have to learn the hard way that others may not share our ideals.

Twelve Angry Men: Sometimes the "majority" simply means all the fools are on the same side.

The Wizard of Oz: Quit waiting for someone to wave a magic wand. Instead, gather a somewhat flawed team about you, attack your problems head-on, and take your destiny into your own hands.

Notice how many of these movies are considered kids' movies? I'll let you (and Robert Fulghum, author of *All I Really Need to Know I Learned in Kindergarten*) draw your own conclusions from this.

In this age of fast food, instant coffee, self-serve gas pumps, and the Internet, we have been trained to become impatient. Indeed, many people now view patience as a vice rather than a virtue. Thus, we hear a lot about instant results and overnight success.

I searched hard for some examples of people who were overnight successes. I ran across a lot of people who were given that label. But if you scratch just beneath the surface of the biography, you will always find years of preparation before the erupting headlines. The singer who is an overnight sensation, other than the fact she studied voice since she was a toddler and worked the club circuit for seven years before recording the big hit. The inventor whose new product is flying off the shelves (but no mention that it took twelve years to develop). The rookie phenom batting .425 his first month in the big leagues, which came after thousands of innings on the ball field since the age of four.

Yes, careers sometimes do emerge from accidents, circumstances, and coincidences. But they can only erupt when you have worked hard, learned your craft, and are poised to jump on those opportunities when they present themselves. You've got to build your product before you can sell it.

3

PERCEPTION EQUALS REALITY

TO DEMONSTRATE HOW IMPORTANT IMAGE IS TO YOUR reputation, let's review two profiles from recent history. Both of these men made silly public mistakes. One man's error was not only ignored, but his statement stands as one of the most inspirational quotes in *Bartlett's Familiar Quotations*. The other man was forever defined by the mistake. The first was John F. Kennedy. The second, former vice president Dan Quayle.

Let's look at President Kennedy, making one of the most inspirational speeches in our history. He stood before the obscene Berlin Wall, denouncing the Communist tyranny that had enslaved the German people. The world was impressed by the bravery, defiance, and dignity of the citizens of West Berlin. Kennedy wanted to express his own admiration and respect by declaring that he stood beside them and considered himself to be one of them. What he wanted to say was, "I am a Berliner." So, speaking in their German language, he announced in dramatic fashion to the wild cheers of a million proud people, *"Ich bin ein Berliner!"* The moment was so dramatic and inspirational that few people noted that Kennedy actually said, "I am a jelly doughnut."

Now let's look at the vice president, who, as Senator Lloyd Bentsen once kindly pointed out, was "no Jack Kennedy." Dan Quayle was on a routine visit to an elementary school. There was a press photo op at which the vice president served as an announcer for a spelling bee. "P-O-T-A-T-O," responded the student. Mr. Quayle gently and quietly told the boy, "You're close, but you left a little something off. The *E* on the end."

The ridicule took on a life of its own as friend, foe, and late-night talk-show hosts alike bemoaned Mr. Quayle's public display of basic spelling disabilities. But, as Paul Harvey would say, let me tell you the rest of the story. Fearing that there might be some tricky or hard-to-pronounce words, the vice president's staff had actually taken the initiative to proofread the cards before the event. They personally reassured Quayle that everything was fine. Despite the precaution, the card the vice president was reading from had an error on it. On it, the word was spelled P-O-T-A-T-O-E.

Now, I am not claiming situational equality here. Certainly a speech in defiance of Communist oppression carries more significance than a comment at a spelling bee. But *because* of the significance, Kennedy was more susceptible to ridicule.

Perhaps that is the point, though. Despite the fact the issue was far more significant, far more somber, and the mistake much sillier, Kennedy was never ridiculed for his error. Quayle, on the other hand, was almost defined by it. So, why is Dan Quayle forever humiliated by this event while John Kennedy gets a pass from critics?

> The way to gain a good reputation is to endeavor to be what you desire to appear.
>
> —Socrates

Because of the image each man had previously built for himself. Kennedy had a long history of precise, inspiring eloquence. As a result, infrequent errors were accepted or ignored. Anyone who pointed out a slip would himself be ridiculed for being nitpicky or having missed the point. Quayle, on the other hand, had cultivated a litany of image-busting mistakes. His gaffes were so numerous that it became a sport to look for them.

Hence, the significant power of image. Perception does indeed become reality, and you need to accept this. This chapter is going to take an unorthodox approach to the subject of image. I may even be accused of handling a serious subject in a frivolous manner. So that you don't get concerned about this alphabetical format just being a gimmick, please note: I picked the subjects and *then* found ways to get them to correspond to the letters, not the other way around. (J, X, and Z were killers.) I'll take your criticism, but make sure you get the point. Developing a positive image is important. People do judge you on small, seemingly trite, impressions.

Image A-Z

Attire

Coco Chanel said that if a woman is poorly dressed, you notice her dress. If she's impeccably dressed, you notice the woman. You should never judge a book by its cover, yet most people do. Likewise, it is wrong to pass judgments about people based on their appearance, but the majority do. Is there anything more important to building your image than the clothes you wear? Sadly, probably not.

We all know of people who are big successes yet look as though they should be sitting in an alley, drinking out of a Woolite bottle. The company president with a bushy beard. The computer entrepreneur who wears only ripped blue jeans. The lawyer with a push-up bra and rainbow makeup. They all succeeded despite themselves. And the key word here is *despite*. They all had talents enabling them to overwhelm their negative image. Or in many cases, the negative image came after they had achieved a high level of success, and they no longer needed to give a rip about what people thought.

Bearers of Bad News

Later in this book we discuss bosses who kill the messenger. That is, they confuse the person bringing the news with the news itself. Interestingly, a lot of people actually relish the idea of putting themselves in this position. You know the types. They slide up to you and tell you about the ridiculous new policies on expense reports, or let you know someone popular is resigning. Or they may even feign a sigh as they report that a new product has failed. And they love to deliver the sad news that a coworker lost a baby or suffered some other horrid tragedy.

Do not be a bearer of bad news. No matter how sincere you are, no matter how helpful and consoling you truly want to be, the fact is that you will forever be associated with that bad news. And if you make a habit of passing along bad news, you will find that people run from you when they see you coming.

Also fitting into this category are those who feel bound to play devil's advocate. People who shoot down the ideas of others, only to hide behind the role of devil's advocate, are just kidding themselves. It is a weak way to fight a battle and will leave your image severely scarred. You will not be remembered as someone who is just putting an idea through due diligence; you will be remembered as "that guy who shot down my project."

Current Events

Would you like to quickly develop an image of being completely out of touch with reality? Then be ignorant of basic current events. Have no idea who won the Super Bowl last night.

Be unaware of the top issue being debated between the Republicans and the Democrats. Have a blank look on your face when someone tries to chat about the latest Court TV drama, a hurricane that just hit Florida, or the controversial nominee for a Best Picture Oscar.

You are certainly not expected to have a deep knowledge of every subject, just an awareness. For instance, sports may hold no interest for you whatsoever, but if you do business in Cleveland, you had better know how the Browns are doing and recognize the name of their quarterback. You may abhor hunting, but if you have clients in Pennsylvania, you should know why people don't answer their phones in November.

Keep in the loop by reading at least one newspaper a day and perhaps a general interest newsmagazine each week. Reading *USA Today* with your morning coffee is good medicine. It covers every subject from serious politics to light banter, and does so in a general, basic manner. (My wife calls *USA Today* the Cliff's Notes of current events.) Daily reading will make you familiar with just about every potential water-cooler topic and keep you from looking like Dan Quayle caught in the headlights.

Desk

Please feel free to have a cluttered desk if you are the CEO or an eccentric scientist, or if you have reached the position you want to retire in. Otherwise, keep your desk clear of anything other than what you are currently working on.

I know, the desk may look cluttered, but you know *exactly* where everything is. Fine, except that to everyone else, you still look like a slob. A cluttered desk sends the message that you are disorganized, and you do not want to cultivate this image.

Embarrassing Moments

Awkward and embarrassing situations happen to everyone. It's a part of life. What you want to avoid is letting these situations take on a life of their own and become a part of your image. Here are some ideas:

- Have a collection of good jokes or anecdotes that you can use whenever there are tense moments. Humor can break the ice when nothing else can. Furthermore, a touch of humor allows people to laugh with you and not at you.
- Don't get flustered or express great distress. Again, most things that we see as embarrassing are rarely even noticed by others. Overreacting to a small event is more harmful to your reputation than the event itself.
- Play the "what-if" game when you are going into a situation that may be awkward. Consider several scenarios, and decide what your reaction will be beforehand. For instance, right now decide what you will do if you grab the wrong water glass at a dinner party, you stumble over a loose carpet, or someone doesn't laugh at one of your jokes.
- Always laugh at other people's jokes. Most people can't tell funny stories well and are greeted with silence. This is humiliating. (Believe me.) You will be a hero in the eyes of these people if you bail them out during these times.
- Never call attention to other people's embarrassments. You may be tempted to do this as a power play, but it will backfire. You will be labeled as a bully or a bore.

First Impressions

There is a terrific episode of *King of the Hill* in which Hank was a loyal Bush supporter until the day he discovered that the then governor had a wimpy handshake. Hank was thoroughly disillusioned that his fellow Texan could have such a disability, and he wandered into the Mexican desert to deal with his grief.

Satire springs from cold truths. A simple handshake is a small part of a first impression, but I use it to illustrate this important point. First impressions stick and may define you forever. Sociologists call this the *primacy effect*. This is the process by which our first impression filters our interpretation of all future behavior in a manner consistent with that first impression. Know this and be alert to all situations you face daily. Meeting a new client. Starting a new job. Being introduced to the boss's husband. Bumping into someone at the supermarket. Always be prepared to make a strong first impression.

> You're never fully dressed without a smile.
>
> —Little Orphan Annie

So, how do you make a great first impression? Again, whole books have been written on this, but I'll give you one word that will take care of the whole issue:

Smile.

Here's why. Smiling conveys two critical things about you—confidence and happiness—and one important thing about the other person—acceptance. Everyone wants to be associated with confident, happy people. And everyone wants to be accepted. These are powerful traits to deploy on a first impression and can by themselves win this person over as a strong ally. Ponder the incredible power of this very simple act, and you will have mastered the art of making a dynamic first impression.

Grammar

Grammar is the clothing of the spoken word. You can be labeled as ignorant with the misuse of a couple of words. Now,

I'm not talking about using the word *whom* correctly—in fact, using that word at all may actually get you labeled as a snob. But do attempt to avoid some of the more common issues. Learn when to say "you and I," and when to say "you and me." Know that there are no such words as *irregardless* or *heighth*. When you write, know the difference between *its* and *it's*. The same with *imply* and *infer*. And I cannot tell you how many times I have heard educated people destroy their image by saying, "I seen . . ."

Humble Yourself

Let me solve once and for all one of the great debates: Should a secretary get coffee for her boss? The answer is *absolutely yes*. Of course, the boss should get coffee for her secretary too. The fact is, whenever one of them is headed to the coffeepot, she should always offer to pick up a cup for the other.

Silly stuff, I know. But some folks soil their image by believing image is enhanced by refusing to do dirty work or menial tasks. The opposite is true. Your image is enhanced every time you humble yourself. Unjam the copy machine, even if you didn't break it. Wipe up a spill on the floor. Change a lightbulb. Make the coffee when the pot seems low. There is nobility in service.

Integrity

There are people who destroy the entire perception of their character by cheating at penny-ante poker, taking a five-foot putt as a gimme, or keeping the extra dollar when a clerk gave the wrong change. I have fired more people for slightly exaggerating an expense report than for incompetence.

Integrity is demonstrated in the small things. Few people, no matter what their character, will ever be tempted to steal a million dollars. But a person's true character is displayed several times a day as he is tempted with small challenges. Little lies, hypocritical actions, forgotten promises—these are the things that will destroy trust. You will lose your reputation for integrity and never get it back.

Just Be Nice

Basic courtesy and simple respect often seem to be fading traits. I still retain the image of a prominent businessman who was yelling—yes, *yelling*—at an airline representative who had just announced that our flight was being delayed. His behavior was not only mean; it wasn't rational. The representative had a good comeback, though: "Sir, at this moment there are only two people in this world who care about your problem, and one of them is quickly losing interest."

It is truly amazing how many people think that they look big and powerful by dumping on "the little people." Discourtesy to an assistant. Snapping at a waiter. Rudeness to a salesclerk. Throwing keys at the valet. Fortunately, these people will get their just desserts; eventually, they will show disrespect to someone they think is a peon who turns out to be the client's wife.

> Your image is enhanced every time you humble yourself. There is nobility in service.

Actually, they'll get their rewards sooner than that. People notice you when you are rude to perceived inferiors. They also notice you when you bestow respect on individuals—regardless of their perceived status—just because they are fellow human beings.

Keeping Confidences

Most people are proud of the fact that they can keep a confidence. "Your secret is safe with me," they will remind you. Of course, they have a dear friend who can also be relied on to keep confidences, so they feel free to share your secret with him. Funny thing, that friend also has a good friend . . .

You will be burned whenever you break a confidence. It will come back to bite you. Being known for an ability to keep private information to yourself is a powerful image. Breaking that trust creates an image that is just as powerful, but in a negative way.

Late, Late, Late!

I had a boss who had a terrible reputation for being late to meetings. While the rest of us steamed and thumb-twiddled, my boss thought nothing of his lateness. In fact, he didn't even recognize the issue. "I'm never late," he would state, "because the meeting never starts until I get there." How presumptuous.

There is no such thing as being fashionably late in business. People resent being asked to wait for you. Being late for meetings or appointments, keeping people waiting on you, is always an image killer. It demonstrates your lack of organization. Most of all, you will earn the reputation for having no respect for other people.

Manners

Let me tell you about a frightening moment I face each day. It is when I arrive at a door a half step before a young woman. If I open the door for her and allow her to precede me, I run a fifty-fifty chance of being told, "I'll open my *own* doors, thank you," implying that I am a chauvinist pig. Of course, if I rush ahead and precede her, most people observing would consider me a rude, unrefined, discourteous rube.

> Beware of people that put numbers after their names.
>
> —Forrest Gump

What to do? Why don't we just cut each other some slack? Gentlemen, continue to treat ladies with courtesy; just don't make a big, sappy deal out of it. Ladies, don't read any more into the gesture than what there is. The guy is trying to be polite, not place you in a subservient position.

The basics of business etiquette were taught to us quite effectively in kindergarten. The rules have not changed. You may want to brush up on assuring yourself that you're grabbing the correct fork or water glass, but don't stress out on trying to figure out how you should behave in the modern world. The trick here is not to learn something new; it is to simply practice what you already know.

> Your middle name has only two purposes. First, it was a way for your mother to let you know that you were in big trouble. The other use of your middle name is for your inauguration as president.

Being courteous, showing respect, and being subservient to guests and coworkers are all traits that you want ascribed to you. You want to have an image of, well, good manners. So what if you are criticized for being too polite? I just wish that was the worst thing people said about me.

Name

Bubba, Skip, Slappy, and other childhood nicknames must be shed by the time you enter college. No matter how socially effective they were as a teenager or in the army, nicknames just don't work in the business world.

Also, save your formal name for funeral notices and wedding invitations. Using it for routine business matters is pretentious. Notice what the ultrasuccessful people call themselves? *Fred* Smith. *Sam* Walton. *Bill* Gates. *Jimmy* Carter. Not Frederick, Samuel, William, or James. (What about *Donald* Trump? Proves my point; he's a bit pretentious, isn't he?)

Your middle name has only two purposes. First, it was a way for your mother to let you know that you were in big trouble. You knew the wrath of God approached whenever she screamed, "Matthew *Jacob*!" The other use of your middle name is for your inauguration as president. Otherwise, reduce it to an initial (formal situations) or omit it altogether.

Office Décor

You will probably spend more time in your office than your home. The urge to customize it is overwhelming. Indeed, you should decorate it in a manner that makes you most comfortable and efficient. Nonetheless, bear in mind that your office will communicate a fair amount about you. Here are some thoughts:

Start with an absolutely vanilla office that completely toes the company line. Let your office décor evolve as you learn the company culture and your coworkers get to know you.

Follow your boss's lead as you begin to customize. No, I do not suggest that you hang pictures of his wife, but observe the things in his office. Some cultures encourage nice art on the walls; others use that space for sales charts.

A couple of family pictures and a tasteful print are good initial additions. Usually, some memorabilia from your favorite college or pro sports team will fit in. Again, let these additions evolve over time. Add them when you can do so without looking over your shoulder or worrying about what others may think.

However, no matter how comfortable you get with the culture, no matter how cozy people feel with you, there are some things to avoid. Never get outlandish, overtly political, or blatantly religious. A picture of you hauling in a trophy fish? OK. Stuffed deer head? Excessive. A photo of you shaking hands with the governor? Good. A *McDavis for President* poster? No. An inspirational religious quote on your desk? Entirely proper. An open Bible lying in the visitor's chair? No.

And never a Confederate battle flag. Especially if you live in a northern state.

Picking Your Flock

Timeless clichés: Birds of a feather flock together. You can tell the character of a man by the company he keeps. That crowd all runs in the same gutter.

You will be perceived in the same image as those with whom you associate. This works for you and against you. It is easy to get associated with the wrong crowd—they actually recruit members. Gathered around the coffeepot or in the corner of the lunchroom, these people are barely hanging on to their jobs, and they use every breath to gripe, backstab, and complain. They will try to draw you into their nattering network of negativism. Join their club, and your career crumbles. Walk briskly away from destructive people.

On the other hand, you can bask in the aura of success and be considered someone on the fast track just by being associated with those who actually are. This is easy to do; golden people are eager to expand their network. Just schedule lunch appointments with the golden people on a regular basis and get to know them. You will adopt their image by osmosis.

Let me add this personal observation: *you become your environment*. The fact is, you will eventually reflect the same standards, level of success, and image of the people and situations you choose to be around. This is a case that goes beyond the concept of perception is reality . . . perception *becomes* reality.

Quit Whining

Ted Turner has a great credo: *Never complain, never explain*. This attitude puts you above it all. Your image will be that you

> Never complain about your problems because 80 percent of the people don't care, and the other 20 percent are glad you have them.

will do your best to control circumstances but won't fall prostrate every time things don't go your way. And you are not going to make a bunch of silly excuses when you fall short. Just pick up your marbles and move ahead with the business at hand.

Never complain about your problems because 80 percent of the people don't care, and the other 20 percent are glad you have them. Whining, complaining, and registering excuses will label you as weak and ineffective. Turner's credo may make you look cold at times, but you will develop an image of strength, leadership, and power. Play the cards you are dealt and shut up about it.

Return Your Messages

Here is something I have discovered in corporate hierarchy: the higher one's status, the easier it is to get in touch with him. High-ranking executives are not only more apt to answer their own phones, but they always return phone calls. Notice that lower-level managers, especially bureaucrats, are virtually impossible to get through to. A fascinating psychological study could be done on this, but I'll leave that for another person and time. But for now, ponder this point. Successful people have an image that includes *easy access*. This easy access gives the perception that you are open, have nothing to hide, and are confident enough to be available to everyone.

Sarcasm

Sarcasm is a coward's tool of conflict. It is a way to viciously attack someone while being able to fall back on "I was only joking" if the attack proves unsuccessful. Sarcastic people earn a reputation of being mean and unreasonable. They are feared, but not in a healthy way. It's a lousy image to have.

It takes sincere and exhaustive effort to stop this habit. You may even need to seek psychological assistance as well as enlist the help of your friends and spouse. Is this effort worthwhile? Yes. Sarcasm will cripple your influence and derail your career. I promise.

Thinking on Your Feet

Jerry Seinfeld tells us about a poll that asked people what scared them the most. Public speaking was rated number one, and death was number two. That's right, death was in second place. He observes, "At a funeral, more people would rather be the corpse than deliver the eulogy."

My friend Greg is known for his eloquence. He seems to have the ability to make a quick speech when called upon unexpectedly. I asked him about this amazing talent, and he taught me an important lesson. The fact is, he does *not* have the ability to say brilliant things without notice or preparation. Instead, he just anticipates situations where he might be called upon and already has a few thoughts prepared in his head—just in case.

So, go ahead and memorize a couple of toasts, just in case you are called upon at the next wedding. Outline a prayer if you are singled out at church. Know some things about all the topics that might pop up at your next convention meeting. And commit a couple of multipurpose anecdotes to memory. Do these things and you will become known as someone who can think on his feet, a nice image to have.

Upbeat

"How are you?" "How are things?" "How is business?" The answer to these questions is always "Great!" Always. It doesn't matter who you are talking with; always be upbeat about things. If you respond to these social inquiries in a negative manner, you will look overwhelmed, in-over-your-head, or just not up to the task. Make sure the impression others have of you is that you have things under control and are successful.

Nobody wants to be around a moody, depressed, or ticked-off person. We all seek to be around people who are upbeat and happy. Misery loves company? Hogwash. People migrate toward positive people and run from depressed ones. Keep all responses to social inquiries positive.

Vices

Smoking can destroy your career. Not harm. Destroy. Some companies will arbitrarily eliminate you for any consideration for promotion if you smoke. There is a growing list of companies that will not hire you if you light up—even when you are not at work. I will wager that there is no company—not even R. J. Reynolds—in which smoking will actually *enhance* your career.

It may take a while for you to kick the habit, so let me give you another snippet of critical advice: avoid smoking in public. This may be harder than it sounds. Most buildings have been declared no-smoking zones, and you must go outside to smoke. Smokers tend to cluster in groups just outside the main entrance to the office, on prominent display to visitors, customers, and their bosses. How does this affect your image? Bosses and coworkers see you "on break" several times a day. Customers and clients see you in a rather vulnerable appearance. Avoid this image-reducing scene and keep your smoking in the closet.

Www.email.com

E-mail is now the preferred method of routine communication in many offices. It has replaced conversation as the primary way to talk informally and has usurped hard-copy memoranda as the method of exchanging information in the workplace. So, realize that there is a good chance that many or most coworkers will create their primary impressions of you based on the e-mail they receive from you.

Let this work to your advantage. Write an e-mail with the same care and attention you give to a memo or business letter to a client. Run a full spell-check, proofread to assure proper grammar, and even paginate it to ensure it looks good on the page.

Be aware of the image your e-mail address sends. Be businesslike, not cute. I have received formal résumés from addresses that include *morebeer, howboutthemdawgs, sexybabe,* and *gunrunner.* No matter how dignified an image the résumé builds, it is flushed right down the toilet when I picture the owners of those addresses.

Xenophobia

Your career will hit a thick wall at the first indication of bigotry. Labeling people based on factors unrelated to them specifically is not only socially unacceptable; it's just plain ignorant. And public displays of ignorance will brand you forever; you will not recover. I am not saying that from a moral viewpoint; I'm talking about good business judgment.

> It takes at least six weeks to prepare a good extemporaneous speech.
>
> —Winston Churchill

Your ability to hire workers, build a team, and relate to customers is compromised when viewing people through stereotypes. Not only will you make bad decisions; you will create perceptions about yourself. You will diminish your capabilities and develop an image of total incompetence. (Listen to the whispers: "Can we trust the decisions on a $40 million account to someone who thinks all Muslims are anti-American?")

Please understand that I'm not talking about political correctness. I *abhor* political correctness. I *am* talking about wisdom and basic respect. For instance, it is completely acceptable in today's society to poke fun at Caucasians, people who are overweight, Christians, men, and southerners. (Heck, I'm five for five.) But it is not respectful. It is not intelligent. Even though telling jokes about people like me won't get you fired or labeled a bigot, it will brand you with an image of being mean. You will also exclude yourself from developing important relationships with people who can be of tremendous benefit to your career.

Yuk It Up

When polled about what is the most attractive thing about a man, most women say *a sense of humor*. (This is not, of course, the number one item on men's lists for women.) But here is an important fact: a self-effacing sense of humor takes other issues off the table. If you poke fun at your weight, for instance, it takes that weapon out of your adversary's arsenal. Someone can't make cutting comments about your weight if you have already joked about it. Likewise, if you have some habit or even a disability that makes people uncomfortable, you will immediately put them at ease. By poking gentle fun at yourself, you have proven that it is not a sensitive subject. People will be more comfortable around you.

Zero

I could come up with no topics starting with the letter *Z*. *Zero*. Also, I was unable to find a way to fit in a critical topic: saying thank you. *Zero*. So, this seems to be a natural place to put it, right at the end of this chapter.

Do you want to find an easy way to enhance what people

think of you? Be liberal in your gratitude. People resent being taken for granted and remember when someone shows them appreciation. This is especially true for the little things.

I figure that if the trash cans at Wendy's can say thank you, then so can I.

Here are two hints that will give your thank-yous maximum impact. First, be specific. Don't just tell your receptionist thank you; add, "I really appreciate the way you talk to my clients when they call."

> I figure that if the trash cans at Wendy's can say thank you, then so can I.

Offer thanks when it is least expected. For instance, every few weeks I will have lunch with my daughter at her school. After the meal, I'll walk up to one of the workers and let her know I notice the great job she is doing. "You folks run a great operation here," I might say. "Thank you for the way you taught Katherine how to clean her tray after eating."

Let me add one last note to this discussion. There are a lot of books you could have purchased to help you with your career. *Thank you* for buying this one. I appreciate your placing that trust in me.

4

LISTEN TO YOUR MOM

Mothers are God's way of communicating with His people. They have a way of cutting to the core of reality. They can be folksy about it; they can be spiritual; or they can hand you wisdom like a sharp sword cutting through a French soldier's soufflé. Whatever her style, Mom always puts your long-term interest at heart and has insight even in technical fields beyond her formal education.

I've found that this simple wisdom is not just applicable to personal life; much of her wisdom can be carried over directly to your career. Here are some stories where moms imparted some solid, loving, brilliant common sense.

Know Your Rights

I had just told my mother the most hurtful news I could possibly deliver. My marriage was facing a crisis that couples often face, and divorce seemed imminent. "But I know Louisiana law," I added. "I've got the right to take the kids and every asset we have. I know my rights!"

My mother, who is known for her quiet, rational—even meek—temperament, smashed the platter that she had been drying onto the kitchen floor. Her eyes narrowed and she pointed her index finger into my face as she sternly replied, "Forget about your rights!" I was stunned. I had never seen my mother like that. She continued with words that I'll always remember: "Just because you have the right to do something doesn't mean it is the right thing to do."

> When you choose the lesser of two evils, remember that it is still an evil.
>
> —Max Lerner

Mother took a deep breath and then returned to her typical soft, deliberate voice. "Your agenda right now is not to get revenge or to soothe your feelings, and it certainly isn't to protect your rights. Your only mission is to save your family."

"And how do I do that? How can this possibly be saved? Look at all the things Kim will have to do to make this marriage and family work!" I countered.

"You are focusing on the wrong thing," she replied. "You are looking at building hurdles. You should be creating passageways."

My blood had stopped boiling long enough to begin listening to what she was teaching me. "How?" I asked.

"Here is your focus: Don't build barriers for Kim to come home. Don't make anyone eat humble pie, grovel, or provide a huge mea culpa. Make it so Kim can just come home and start living again. Make it easy to do the right thing. Make it hard to do the wrong thing."

I took that advice, added a lot of praying and counseling, and we did save our family. And a side benefit was a business philosophy that has built my management career: *Make it easy to succeed; make it hard to fail.*

> Just because you have the right to do something doesn't mean it is the right thing to do.

I applied the statement to systems design. I built processes that used the

> The best index to a person's character is (a) how he treats people who can't do him any good, and (b) how he treats people who can't fight back.
>
> —Abigail Van Buren

easiest possible path to success. They made it difficult to get the wrong results. If workers were using shortcuts, I developed processes where the shortcuts led to the correct results instead of disasters. I made it easy to do the process correctly, thus ensuring that the right results were attained more often.

Mom's advice certainly achieved the most important results in my life; it saved my family. But it also was the cornerstone for building a successful career. All in all, that thirty-minute conversation yielded more results than my eighteen years of formal education.

Be Where You Are

We hope that our children observe our wonderful habits and replicate them in their lives forevermore. Experts tell us that a child must see a good habit demonstrated seven times before making it one of her own. And, sigh, they also pick up the bad habits, but they usually don't need to see any repetition to embrace one. And when they see us doing something stupid, they will lock onto it like a pit bull on an intruder's throat.

Katherine showed this to her mom, Tina, during a wonderful break from Tina's job teaching time-management seminars. Tina was on a zippy ride at an amusement park with her daughter. There they were, whirling around in high-speed arcs, defying all laws of physics. (They could do this because neither Katherine nor her mother actually knew any laws of physics.) With the wind in her hair and her eyes open wide, Katherine began a nonstop monologue: "After this, can we ride the roller-coaster? And then go to the Foam Factory? And I want to play golf again, and then go to McDonald's . . ."

Tina stopped her. "Katherine," she said firmly, "stop thinking about things that we can do *later*. Enjoy what we are doing right *now*."

But the problem continued. While they were doing something fun, little Katherine's mind would be on other things or events. That violated one fundamental principle Tina teaches in her time-management seminars: *Be where you are.* If you are in a meeting about plant safety, don't worry about your personal finances. Concentrate all your energies on the activity you are currently involved in. Practicing this is how a person can successfully deal with a plate loaded with responsibilities and activities.

> Laugh at yourself first, before anyone else can.
>
> —Elsa Maxwell

So, how can I teach her this important life lesson? Tina wondered. *Maybe I should put away my cell phone when we're at the playground. Perhaps she shouldn't witness a worried look on my face while I'm thinking about a business problem during dinner. Maybe when she sings "Sally the Camel" I should keep track of the humps on the camel instead of the possibility of snow tomorrow.*

Tina decided she should just enjoy the moment of seeing Katherine play, and color, and sing, and be silly. And then, just maybe, Katherine will also learn to live the moment.

Go Ahead—Burn a Bridge Now and Then

Laura tells of the day her mother said, "I absolutely think you should take the new job, Laura. In fact, you must do it." Laura was more than a little surprised. "I had just told her about an opportunity I was exploring," Laura continued. "After six years as a secretary, I had been offered a job as a marketing representative for a new manufacturing company just opening its doors in Minneapolis. I had spent my whole life avoiding risk, and this move required a gigantic leap of faith.

"My mom's response and enthusiasm surprised me because I had been raised in a family completely averse to risk. My father worked for the post office for forty-two years, my mother was raised on a farm during the Depression, and the only investments either had ever made were in government savings bonds. Her answer was a bit out of character, so I felt I should give her some reassurance: 'Of course, I'm going to give ample notice and see to it that they have a well-trained person to replace me. I don't want to burn any bridges, you know.'

> Many a false step is made standing still.
>
> —Patti LaBelle

"Her next words surprised me even more than her previous declaration. 'Yes, you do,' she said quietly. 'I do, *what*?' I replied. 'You most certainly do want to burn your bridges,' she said while pouring each of us another cup of coffee. I was glad for the additional caffeine, because hearing one of my favorite clichés shot down—by the most security-oriented person on earth—required some type of drug supplement.

"My mom then continued, in her quiet, reasoned voice: 'You have worked far beneath your potential for much too long. This is an opportunity you must take. But like anything else new in life, you will have some initial setbacks, fears, and self-doubts. It'll be hard, but if you keep fighting, you will succeed. But if you have something comfortable to fall back on, you just might be tempted to retreat, to quit, and to go back to your easier life. Your father and I have missed a lot of exciting opportunities in our lives, just because we were too security conscious. Every once in a while you have got to go out on a limb, because that is where all the fruit is.

"'If you fight, you *will* succeed. And if you have no other options, you will make that fight. Laura, if you want to have a great future, go ahead and burn that bridge to the past. That way, you have no choice but to move forward.'"

Ego Growth

As she experienced life, Janet was able to confirm something she once heard her mother state:

"When I was in my twenties, I was always worried about what people were thinking about me. In my thirties, I really didn't care what people were thinking about me. But now that I am forty, I realize that nobody has actually been thinking about me."

Quality Time

Nathalie pulled her car into her mother's driveway at 12:45 sharp. She was returning from her job at the police department, where she worked evenings, processing various citizen complaints that came in during the late hours. Exhausted, she pulled out her key and let herself in, going directly upstairs to her son's makeshift bedroom. The two-year-old lay there asleep, but his eyes halfway opened as he sensed his mother's presence. He quietly said, "Hello, Mama," as Nathalie brushed his long hair from his eyes; then he slowly went back to sleep.

She stuck her head into her mother's room and, knowing she would still be awake, said, "It's me. I'll be taking Joey with me now." "Why don't you just go ahead and stay here tonight?" her mother always asked. And Nathalie replied, as she always did, "No, I'd better be getting him on home." She bundled up the growing boy, strapped him into his car seat, and made the thirty-minute drive to her apartment on the other side of Wichita.

She tucked him into his own bed about 1:30, which was routine. Then she found she was unable to sleep, which was also routine. She lay in her bed and grabbed a celebrity magazine, one of the few luxuries she allowed herself. Money is always tight for a single mom. Joey's father helped out some from time to time, but she really couldn't depend on anything steady. Nathalie's mother—God bless her—did all she could, but she had other children and grandchildren and a life of her own to deal with. So money was tight even with a second part-time job.

> We use 10 percent of our brains. Imagine what we could accomplish if we used the other 60 percent.
>
> —Ellen Degeneres

She zeroed in on an article about the anniversary of the death of a real-life princess. The article focused on what a great mother she was, how, even with her busy life, she made quality time for them. She would visit her children every month at their boarding school and even called them three times a week to listen to their problems. When they were younger, the princess would read to them every night before the nanny tucked them in. Her children mourned her deeply when she was tragically killed in an accident while on vacation. And they still miss her today, the article concluded.

As her eyes finally began to get heavy, Nathalie laid the magazine on the nightstand and turned out the light. She needed to sleep, because she had to go to her part-time job at noon the next day and she wanted to spend a few hours with her son before leaving. He was at the age where he was discovering new things every day. And he always had a unique perspective on the world.

Just last week she was chatting with a friend on the back porch when Joey interrupted them again and again to show his mama a caterpillar, point out an anthill, or ask about an odd noise. "Why do you let him interrupt you so much?" her friend asked. "I brought him into this world," she responded. "I guess I ought to let him show it to me."

Nathalie had found that quality time may have a nice ring to it, but you just can't schedule seeing his first steps, or hearing his first words, or appointments for potty lessons. These things only came by being there as much as possible. If you are, the odds say that you'll witness most of the important events.

This also held true as the child grew older and wanted to talk about his problems, doubts, and concerns. She just couldn't schedule these things for "quality time." She found she needed to be there when he scraped his knee, when he was cut from the basketball team, or when his first crush dumped him. She left work early one afternoon, upon receiving a phone call from Joey about his rejection letter from the university. "I'll be there," she told him, and of course, she was.

Nathalie continued to work two, sometimes three jobs as Joey grew up, yet she was able to arrange her time so that she was there. Sure, she wasn't with him 100 percent. That wasn't possible. But she found that if she made being with her son her top priority, she'd be around for many of the critical times in his life. And she was there during those not-so-critical times too, when nothing was scheduled but important subjects came up nonetheless. It was during these unplanned moments that she spoke of her faith and values, taught him respect for others, and educated him on what it means to be a good citizen and neighbor. "Thank God I was there," she found herself saying over the years. "Thank God I was there for him when he needed someone."

Nathalie wept with pride when Joey was awarded his badge as

the newest member of the Wichita Police Department. He was assigned a post in community relations, working with young boys and girls who were destined for trouble without an adult's intervention. Joey sponsored basketball games and homework labs, but he found that he seemed to do the most good as they all just hung out. The youth began spilling their guts while chewing on a pizza or just shooting the breeze on the sidelines.

He found great success in shaping that newest generation. And he will tell you today that his success came during impromptu times, not during an organized activity. Just because he was there when the kids needed to talk.

When Joey was studying to take the sergeant's exam, he took a business class that promoted a concept called "Management by Wandering Around." It seemed like a great management style, but it gnawed at him that he had heard it all before.

And indeed he had.

When I completed the first draft of this book, I printed off a copy and traveled to Memphis to present it to my mother. Mom had recently celebrated her eightieth birthday in the hospital. I had dedicated the book to her and wanted her to see it.

We visited for several hours that evening, and I read her passages from the book. She smiled at some of the stories, recognized the source of a lot of my advice, and especially appreciated those anecdotes inspired by my youngest daughter, Katherine.

Let me tell you a little bit about my mother. Blanche Baggett grew up in Mississippi during the Great Depression. In 1931, her father died in the drought-burned fields of their small family farm, leaving my mom and her baby sister to be cared for by their young mother. My uncle, then twelve years old, became the man of the house and capably filled this role until called to fight in the war. Mom, her sister, and my grandmother then did what all the women in America did during that crisis: they assured our country's survival. They produced the needed goods and services, preserved its homes, and were the backbone of its spirit and moral fiber.

All of my mother's family survived—triumphed over—those amazing years. Mom went on to marry a veteran, raise two children, face many more life crises, and quietly impart her amazing wisdom, character, and deep faith to everyone she touched. It is this transfer of wisdom that led me to write this chapter as well as dedicate this book to her.

I was at the softball field watching Katherine throw a ball from third (almost) to first when my cell phone rang. My father's soft voice cracked as he told me my mother had peacefully passed away that morning.

So Mom never got to see the nice, professionally produced book you are now holding in your hands. But she did get to see the words. She got to hear me read her stories, many of which she inspired. And she did know how deeply grateful her son was for helping shape his life and for her role in making this country what it is today.

Use this moment as your opportunity to reminisce about the very real principles your mom blesses you with. She is your best education.

Section II

MATURE YOUR CAREER

5

DEVELOP RELATIONSHIPS

In the Introduction, I told you about an amazing event I attended just out of high school. For one incredible week, I chatted with, asked questions of, and listened to lectures by some of the greatest men and women of the time. One speaker was Sam Battistone, president of one of the country's largest restaurant chains. He was asked, "How do you get to be president of a major corporation when you are only thirty-one years old?" His answer had us all riveted:

> When I was eight years old, I mopped floors and cleaned tables in one of my dad's restaurants, and when I was ten I washed maybe a thousand dishes a night. When I was sixteen, I managed one of my dad's restaurants, and by the time I was eighteen, I was working a hundred hours a week overseeing a dozen of them. I served long hours working in real estate, marketing, and even the finance department, giving up the social activities that a normal twenty-year-old would have just so I could make my father's company the strongest one in the industry.
>
> You want to know how to be the president of a major company by the time you are thirty-one? Get yourself a father who owns a chain of restaurants.

No matter how hard you work, how smart you are, or how lucky you may be, you can become successful only through the association and cooperation of other people. As the turtle sitting on the fencepost said, "I don't know how I got here, but I am pretty sure I didn't do it all by myself."

Most of us are not like Sam. We don't have a family member ready to reward us for our hard work. We have to cultivate this collection of promoters. In other words, we've got to build a network.

Networking

Only in America can we morph *making business friends* into a technical skill called *building a network*. We've overcomplicated just about everything else, so why not this?

I fear that the term *networking* has taken the very important task of developing relationships and turned it into a cold, impersonal task of Rolodex building. As with many other topics, you can find the bookshelves filled with how-tos on this subject. In fact, the current definition of networking has evolved to resemble the opening scene from *The Godfather*. After receiving a favor from the godfather, the young man is told, "Some day, and that day may never come, I will call upon you to do me a service in return. Until that day, consider this justice a gift." It is a business transaction. Our relationship is designed to exchange favors, and we must keep the ledger balanced.

I'm going to avoid the instruction these books give. Instead, I want to concentrate on the more positive and fruitful aspects represented by networking's first cousin, *relationship building*.

Relationship Building: What Networking Should Be

Sometimes the networking process seems insincere, artificial, and cold. Networking parties take on all the charm of a Broadway cattle call. Lots of folks shining their best smiles, trying to make rehearsed dialogue sound spontaneous, while ensuring that the new network contact has their business card. Ugh.

That's really not how it should be. Build your network through genuine associations and friendships.

Public relations consultant Ralph Reed probably has one of the most extensive networks in the country. That network includes members of Congress, governors, billionaires, and even presidents. It also includes janitors, reporters, midlevel managers, and students. Listen to his perspective on what he calls friendship building:

> Career building is really friendship building. In our work, our personal lives, and our hobbies and avocations, friends are the currency of life. Make friends, build relationships, and be a friend to others by helping them in every way you can.
>
> This is different than just "networking"; it is really getting to know others, helping others, and being there to make a phone call, drop a line, or make a recommendation for them as well.
>
> At least once a day, I try to help someone who I have no reason to believe can ever help me. It might be a kind e-mail, a referral, or a recommendation, but it matters to help others, particularly when you expect nothing in return.
>
> Successful people—not just as the world defines them, but in the values of life that really matter—are friends first.

Where to Make Friends

Good networking simply refers to developing friends, business relationships, and contacts who will help you in your career. The relationship is more intimate than a Rolodex association, though usually not exactly a personal friendship.

> It's always smart to learn from your mistakes. It's even smarter to learn from the mistakes of others.
>
> —Hillel Segal

So, skip the networking parties and the insincere business-card exchanges. To develop these relationships, you simply have to go where the people you want to know congregate. Here are some suggestions:

Professional associations. Every industry has a trade association or professional group. These range from informal affairs to structured groups like the American Bar Association and the American Medical Association. If you are new to networking, this is a great place to get started. You will be mixing with people you can relate to. You will learn about other organizations and the opportunities available within them. You may even find out about new openings before they are made public, and you will keep up with competitive developments.

Religious groups. Many local churches and synagogues sponsor business groups and services, especially career-development programs. Attending these programs provides the added bonus of working with people who share your values.

Colleges and schools. I have a good friend who is a superior court judge. I met him when he was teaching a business law class that I took at a local college. Taking courses in your field is a great way to meet peers and leaders in your field of interest. Stay after class and chat with a classmate or invite someone for a cup of coffee.

Political groups. Nobody networks like politicians. You will find it incredibly simple to blend into a political group and feel welcome. These associations are eager to recruit active members. Like religious associations, political groups offer the opportunity to be with people who share your values and beliefs. Note that political associations are not limited to political parties; get involved in any cause that you feel passionate about.

Also, get to know your local representatives, council members, and state senators. They, and their staffs, are quite interested in developing a relationship with you, and you will find it easy to become part of their network.

Volunteer Activities. Please don't consider me shallow for listing this as a networking tool. Certainly, the primary reason for volunteering is to help the cause you choose to support. But do not overlook the career benefits of volunteering. Get to know the board of directors for the organizations you work with. Who do you think sits on these boards? Usually company presidents, key executives, bank presidents, and other influential business leaders.

If you really want to get your name known by key people, volunteer for fund-raising. You'll be talking to some key executives for local corporations, and they'll be getting to know you while you are clothed in the cloak of their favorite civic or charitable organization.

Grow Your Relationships

So much emphasis is placed on collecting business cards that we are rarely told how to maintain and grow our relationships. Actually, filling a Rolodex is the easy part. Nurturing the friendships is where the real reward comes in.

You nurture your network in the same manner in which you nurture friendships. OK, it is true that a business network is not as close as a personal friendship (for instance, I do not share my personal problems with people in my network), but both require genuineness and warmth.

Send greeting cards liberally. Holiday greetings are a must. But also look for other opportunities to stay in touch with your business friends. Read the newspaper with a pair of scissors in your hand. Send articles that may be of interest to your network; they'll be flattered that you were thinking of them. Actually, there is a twenty-first-century way to do this now: using the Internet. Go to google.com and navigate to the news page. You can type in a keyword, and it will deliver newspaper articles (from more than one hundred newspapers nationwide) that include that keyword. Set up a few keywords for each network member, and run searches each month. It's easy to forward an article to your business friends, and they will be grateful for your attention.

> Keep away from people who try to belittle your ambitions. Small people always do that, but the really great make you feel that you, too, can become great.
>
> —Mark Twain

One other important thing to remember in growing your relationships is to remember the kids. When people remember me, they have my attention. When they remember my children, they have my devotion. Keep a list of the hobbies and interests of each person's children. An occasional birthday card, an article about soccer, and a letter of recommendation to a college are powerful ways to deepen your relationship with those in your network.

Mentoring

A mentor is a role model who takes a personal professional interest in you. He or she might trade e-mails each day, have lunch once a week, or just chat sporadically through the year. A mentor can teach you who's who in an organization and how you should approach people. Seasoned professionals offer guidance to aspiring careerists. Female executives help other women crack the glass ceiling. Wise alumni take uncertain young graduates under their wings.

There are a lot of political land mines in any organization. Mentors can help you with turf issues, politics, knowing what to say to whom and when. They help you figure it all out. And they go to bat for you if someone misconstrues what you say.

I Gotta Get Me One of These

The toughest part of a mentoring relationship is finding a mentor. Consider these tips:

- Don't be afraid to approach someone. Almost everyone, especially at a senior level, understands the importance of mentoring. Because of this, you may find that the more successful a person is, the more receptive she will be to your inquiry. Most successful people are genuinely interested in helping others succeed.
- Be a bit subtle in your approach. For instance, I'd probably recoil if someone were to approach me and say, "Will you be my mentor?" But I would be flattered if he said, "Can I bounce some ideas off you from time to time? I could use your advice."
- Avoid arranged "marriages." While their intention is pure, company programs that assign mentors usually don't work. You have the best chance of success if you discover each other through networking or introduction by an acquaintance.
- Know what you want from the relationship. Understand your purpose and the results you seek. Know your needs,

and then track down the person who can best provide them. This clarity also eliminates any future confusion regarding roles and expectations.

- Understand that while there are advantages to having a mentor with a background similar to yours, you may be enriched by having a diverse pool of mentors. Talk to someone with a similar background *and* someone who is not from that background. You may get different suggestions and viewpoints.
- Keep it business. There is a natural urge to allow the business advice to become personal guidance. You are not seeking a father, therapist, or minister. These are separate relationships. A mentor serves a specific business purpose. You must keep the borders guarded to assure that the business benefits don't get diluted.
- Choose a member of the same sex. There are too many opportunities for misunderstandings otherwise. And sometimes the problems become worse than misunderstandings. Let's face it, mentoring often leads to a close, personal relationship, and the lines can become fuzzy. You don't want to ruin a great mentorship opportunity by creating a crisis.
- Make sure your values are aligned. If you detest playing games and backstabbing, you will be in a mess of trouble by having a mentor who plays dirty politics.
- Keep an open mind. A mentor is someone who will help you grow in the areas most important to you. Look for someone who exemplifies the *traits and skills* that you want to adopt, not the exact career path. For instance, if you are an accountant who lacks some social skills, you may find that a great salesman would be a more appropriate mentor than a CFO.

- Don't try to have a mentor relationship with your supervisor or anyone in your chain of command. There are too many opportunities for conflict and confusion about roles. Often you will want to ask, "Did you just tell me that as my boss or my mentor?" The roles are different and the relationship is complex. Don't add further confusion to the mix.
- Realize that the mentor doesn't have to be older, but that is usually best. Don't get too outside the box on this. While it is possible that someone your age or even younger could serve as a positive mentor, the odds oppose it. Be conventional and enlist someone who has had a generation of experience to pass along to you.

Do you want to make friends? Be friendly.

—Dale Carnegie

I questioned her lyrics the first time I heard Barbra Streisand sing her hit song "People." She sang: "People who need people are the luckiest people in the world." *Shouldn't it be "People who don't need people"?* I thought. But no, Streisand actually got this one right. We not only need people in our lives, we are quite fortunate to have that need.

Whether it is a parent, schoolmate, neighbor, spouse, coworker, boss, mentor, or any other role, relationships are absolutely critical to success. This need feeds our careers because it *requires* us to involve others in our growth and evolution. The harvesting of ideas, opinions, and perspectives make us stronger and our careers more dynamic.

Careers cannot be solo acts. And that is a good thing.

6

DON'T SCREW UP

JUST AFTER SURVIVING THE GREAT FLOOD OF 1990, MY COUSIN Ralph attended an old-fashioned tent revival one hot, sticky southern evening. The preacher had them whooped into a frenzy on the subject of sin and forgiveness. Person after person would take the microphone and confess their pagan ways, followed by the congregation clapping and cheering for their repentance. People would tearfully confess to cheating and drinking and stealing and just about every other country music topic, and the congregation would shout their encouragement and sing and cry in support.

Finally, Cousin Ralph stood by his seat and confessed a recent sin. The congregation became completely silent, their mouths dropped open, and their faces turned a whiter shade of pale. The preacher looked up at Ralph and said, "Brother, I don't think I would have told that one."

Businesses become successful not by doing things right, but by not doing things wrong. The absence of negatives is often much stronger than the possession of some brilliant positive. An example? Look at the fast-food industry. Research determined what the customer most wants from a fast-food place. Is it quality? Way down the list. Cleanliness? Important, but not at the top. How about price? Actually not. The thing that a customer most wants to tell fast-food places is this: "Don't screw up my order."

> Of all sad words of tongue or pen, the saddest are these: "It might have been!"
>
> —John Greenleaf Whittier

Some careers are like that. You can build a solid, progressive career in many companies and industries by simply being there, providing steady services, and not doing bad things. The old joke is, "Around here, one *oh brother!* erases a thousand *attaboys*."

Do not interpret the scientific term *screwups* with failure. Indeed repeated failures are screwups, but we are not focusing on the positive career-building strategy of taking calculated risks. No, when I say, "Don't screw up," I am referring to social, political, and character faux pas that are usually the outgrowth of unplanned and unthinking idiocy.

While there are certainly a myriad of events that can derail your career, most of them are logical. All the things you are warned about in your employee handbook can slam the door in your face, but most people reading this book have advanced well past the stage where these items are an issue. There are some items, however, that might not be as obvious as those covered in kindergarten. If your career has hit a silent roadblock, chances are you can find the reasons on these next few pages.

Career Killers

Neglecting to Keep Skills Updated

Some people stop learning when they attain the job of their dreams. They thought of education only as a tool for getting them where they were going. These people are destined for being displayed in a museum as the fossils they truly are. I'm not talking about you, of course. You're smart enough to follow the lead of physicians and schoolteachers who know that they must learn constantly simply because the world is changing so quickly. The world has seen many a wunderkind melt into obsolescence just because he thought that the knowledge that got him there was good enough to keep him there. Keep yourself on a constant, steady, up-to-the-minute training program throughout your career.

Now, what does "training program" mean? Sure, formal programs play an important role. It is often wise to get an advanced degree, particularly if most new people coming in at your level seem to have them. Also, formal programs include those offered by your company or through career associations. CPAs and teachers' associations are good about offering excellent career-maintaining courses.

But don't overlook informal training or skills you learn on your own. Look at noncredit courses offered by local colleges. They do not have to be strictly related to your field to advance your career. For instance, people in every profession can benefit from courses in consumer law, business writing, and accounting. Your informal training program should also include regular reading of business books, trade journals, and magazines. The point is that you must broaden your view of ongoing education to include things beyond formal degree programs. You must take charge of your advancement and take advantage of all learning opportunities.

Another key point in your ongoing education is the ability to spot new trends. Keep an eye out for new skills that may become commonplace in your industry. A perfect example of this is the computer. Just twenty years ago, computer skills were the exclusive jurisdiction of a narrow slice of the workforce, usually housed in an air-conditioned room in the basement. Today a computer sits on every desk and in the bedrooms of most seven-year-olds.

When I entered the workforce, typing your own letters meant you were at the bottom of the pecking order and didn't rate your own secretary. Today there are no secretaries.

There probably aren't any technologies on the horizon that will have the general impact that the computer has had, but there are probably changes afoot that will have just as revolutionary an impact on your specific industry.

David is a mechanical designer at a major consumer products company. He offers this strategy:

> I have worked at the same company for twenty-four years. When I began, all the drawings were done by hand with pencil and paper. Then 2D CAD—computer-aided design—workstations were introduced. My company installed only a few of these workstations and most of the other designers avoided using them, choosing instead to stick with the pencil and gadgets that had served them well their whole careers. I took a different approach and embraced this new design technology. Inevitably, the company hit a rough patch and had a "reduction in force." I and the others who had learned the 2D CAD were retained. The others were laid off.

Spot technology and systems changes early and become fluent in their use. Staying ahead of the curve will propel your career. Failure to do so will return you to the days of carbon paper.

Misusing Authority

I rewrote this section four times. First, I included a story of a top executive I knew who lost everything. Not just his career, everything. I deleted this because it just seemed too melodramatic, and I thought my readers would mumble, "That would never be me."

I replaced that with another story, but it came across too preachy, and the log in my eye is too large for me to be preaching to anyone about the splinter in his. Then I got really frustrated with the text I replaced *that* with. I finally figured out why the section wasn't working. It's because the crime and the consequences were just too obvious. Some things don't need to be explained.

> Rank is responsibility, not privilege.
>
> —Peter Drucker

Yet I can say unequivocally that the number one reason I have ever fired anyone is for misuse of authority. More than stealing, incompetence, and insubordination combined. Now, that may just be the real story of this chapter. The single biggest reason for getting fired is for doing something that the person knew was forbidden before he or she did it.

What is meant by "misuse of authority"? It is using power given to you by your company in order to attain personal things. Sexual harassment is the most dominant example. But granting unauthorized merchandise discounts, giving unearned jobs to friends, giving unfair perks to yourself, having employees run family errands, and controlling an employee's personal life are just as prevalent.

Power is granted for accomplishing objectives that assist the corporation in meeting its goals. Using it for your own objectives is morally criminal.

Rats. Still too preachy.

Refusing Accountability

Responsibility equals authority. You are responsible for everything you have authority over. And you will eventually be given authority for everything you accept responsibility for. Let that soak in. Your power will diminish each time you declare that something is not your responsibility. And your power will increase every time you accept responsibility for something—even when that "something" is a mistake or a failure.

The quickest way up the career ladder is to claim responsibility—ergo, authority. The fastest way down the ladder? Make it a point to claim that something is not your fault. Remember, a manager secure enough to admit her shortcomings, as well as develop a solution to the problem, shows maturity and leadership.

News Item: Squarehole Corporation Fires Mr. Roundpeg

My wife dragged me to a chick flick. While the primary message of this movie was, of course, that men are basically evil, it did make an attempt to convey an additional plot line.

Julia Roberts plays a young, beautiful, free-spirited art teacher hailing from Hollywood, who captures a teaching position at an ultraconservative women's college on the East Coast during the height of the Eisenhower administration. Understand that half the women at this college are married before they graduate and the other half within a month thereafter. Classes are taught in motherhood, and the school nurse is fired for discussing birth control. Yet the new art teacher tosses aside the syllabus on classics and great masters and unveils Picasso and Jackson Pollock. And—get this—the prehippie from Tinseltown is shocked—*shocked!*—to discover that she is met with resistance to her new ways.

> If you wouldn't want to see your actions described on the front page of your hometown newspaper, don't do it.
>
> —Walter J. Wadsworth

Hollywood is quite prolific in churning out movies like this. (Interestingly, three Robin Williams films come to mind—*Patch Adams*; *Good Morning, Vietnam*; and *Dead Poets Society*.) A liberal-minded individual is placed in a conservative setting and then fights to completely overhaul the system, all the while amazed that he or she would face any conflict. The usual outcome of these movies is that, while beaten down, the hero is not defeated, and there is some modicum of change in the institution.

While this plot line offers the opportunity for good film drama, it is poor career instruction. It just doesn't happen like that in real life. Yes, it is absolutely true that one person can change a company culture—if that person is the CEO or owner of the company. But one person cannot change the culture from middle management or at the bottom. And the new guy can never change it.

Unless it is the top job, do not go to work for a company that does not reflect your values. You will not be able to change, and it is an absolute fact that they never will. Conflict is inevitable, and you will be the loser.

Understand that this advice is offered even if you have no intention of changing the company. Failure is your destiny even if you decide to keep your mouth shut and go along. The company will not adapt to your values, and neither will you be able to live with its.

Hanging with the Wrong Crowd

As previously discussed, you are identified with the company you keep. Every department has a clutch of people who huddle together after meetings, during lunch, and after work, whose universal focus is to gripe. These people are poison. Even if you do not participate, you will be identified with every comment this group makes. When it comes time for layoffs, I assure you that this fraternity will sink together. If you have shared space with these people, you are given membership in that fraternity.

Punting on Promises

Several times in this book I speak of how important it is to your career to seek out and accept responsibility. Indeed, having the reputation for taking responsibility is a powerful image to create. But that is not the whole story. The fact is that accepting responsibility is easy. Delivering results is the hard part.

Eager-to-please executives often stumble into the muddy pit of overcommitment. They volunteer for every project imaginable, and trouble follows. Balls are dropped, confidence wanes, and their reputation rots. Being known as unreliable will result in deep, permanent battle scars. Limit your projects to those on which you will do a solid job and deliver on time.

Being a Perfectionist

Notice that the last sentence said to do a "solid" job. Not exceptional. Not perfect. Just solid. Holding out for perfection will result in never achieving your goal and producing few projects. The pursuit of perfectionism (by definition, having zero screwups) is in itself a dramatic screwup. Hey, quit trying to reconcile the theory and just understand the concept. Mistakes and hiccups and less-than-perfection are not screwups. Low production and overly complicated solutions are.

Being a Little Bit Dishonest

In a recent study by the Corporate Leadership Council, the top characteristics of effective leadership were "honesty and integrity"—ahead of inspiring others, having a long-term strategy for the future, and communicating expectations clearly.

If you fall short on the qualities of honesty and integrity, you are no doubt having trouble influencing people to your point of view. You may be trying to blame others for things you should be taking responsibility for.

It is amazing how easy it is to lose the trust of others. You do not have to be convicted of embezzlement to have this stigma attached to you. How many people have lost their jobs because they fudged an expense report by five dollars? How many more people have had their reputations silently damaged because it simply *looked* as though they played with the expense account numbers?

Let me add something here. Suspicion of wrongdoing does just about as much harm as wrongdoing itself. Protect yourself when you are in innocent situations that could be wrongly interpreted. If you show up for a business meeting in a hotel room with someone you have never met before, and it turns out that someone is of the opposite sex, immediately relocate the meeting to the lobby. If you are sitting near a group of people snickering about manipulating sales data, get up and move to the other side of the room so no one will think you are part of the group. Attach receipts for all your expenses, even if policy does not require receipts for under ten dollars. You get the idea. Build your reputation for integrity as carefully as you would competency on a résumé.

Posterior Mastication Maximus

There are times when you are "guilty." Maybe not of a crime, but of a big career mistake. Perhaps you fudged an expense account. Maybe there was an improper relationship. Maybe you were caught in a conflict-of-interest issue. My hope is that you will live your life and career without ethical blemish, but if this is not the case, you do not need to be sentenced to execution. How do you survive this?

The conclusion does not necessarily have to be inevitable. Much of the time, your continued tenure is determined not by what you did, but by how you handle it.

Settle Early

Cut your losses early, and you'll have the best chance for survival. It wasn't the break-in at Watergate that sank Richard Nixon; it was the cover-up. Bill Clinton's greatest blunder? Making the statement, "I never had sexual relations with that woman." And note that Martha Stewart was not convicted of insider trading; she was convicted of lying to investigators.

The more the "prosecutor" has to invest in your case, the more flesh he will want to extract. Let's use the example of a faulty expense report. Fight it, deny it, and force the auditor to build an airtight case against you, and you will be fired.

Today a Peacock, Tomorrow a Feather Duster

Put your hat in your hand, go see your boss, and confess that you shouldn't have listed that dinner, and you were absolutely wrong to do it; chances are you will live to see another day, albeit with your pants fitting a bit more loosely in the back. Be objective enough to recognize when the sky really is about to fall, and quickly conjure up sufficient contriteness.

The rules of boxing state you never hit a man when he is lying on the mat. Hunters do not shoot doves while the birds are feeding in a field. And bears don't attack prey lying motionless on the ground. It works the same way when you are called on the carpet. *Stay* on the carpet and do not argue. Don't even clarify errors. The carnage will soon stop when it becomes obvious that you are not defending yourself. It will evolve into a civilized conversation where you can make your points calmly and with the proper level of contriteness.

> It's not an apology if the words *I'm sorry* are followed by the word *but*.

Make certain you include these two words: *I'm sorry.* While these words are not enough in themselves, they are essential for you to survive. Your boss will assume that if you are truly sorry, there is a good chance you will not repeat the act. Conversely, if you are not sorry, there is a strong probability that you will repeat it; only next time you'll do it in a manner that you won't get caught. And remember this bit of advice: it's not an apology if the words *I'm sorry* are followed by the word *but.*

Anticipate a Positive Outcome

Explain that you know what you did was wrong. Add, "I'll not try to explain why I did it; that would only make it sound like I'm trying to justify it. And I'm not. I was wrong, period." Then add, "Let me tell you what I intend to do to rectify the situation and, more important, assure you that you will never have to worry about me doing anything like this again." Then lay out a detailed plan that includes the proper apologies and actions needed to justify your continued employment.

This may not work. The act may be so egregious as to eliminate any chance of rehabilitation. Or the company's managers may simply have their minds made up before you walk into the room. So be it; there is no downside to trying. And if you do get fired, your response may soften the impact on your terms for leaving. They may let you resign, let you keep certain benefits, or even offer a good recommendation.

Surviving Land Mines

I was once an officer of a small company that eventually merged with another company and grew into a well-known national corporation (long after I worked there). I saw that corporation in the news a while ago in a headline-grabbing scandal, as some of its top officers were accused of corruption. Some of them are now in jail; others are awaiting a high-profile trial.

While I did not personally know anyone who was indicted, I did know several people who saw their lives dragged through the mud and careers destroyed by association.

These are good, decent men, but their public image is forever polluted because of their association with this mess. Their lawyers have kept them out of jail, but their reputations are destroyed. I'm not sure if this is really a victory.

Lawyers have one goal in mind: to keep their clients out of jail. Many lawyers consider that as the only measure of victory, no matter what the other consequences. But that may not be a total victory for you if your career and reputation are destroyed in the process. Sometimes preserving your career or reputation requires accepting a certain amount of risk.

For instance, let's assume you are a CFO for a corporation. You are (unfairly) accused of wrongdoing. Let's say that you are accused of misstating expenses and revenue. Not only are you about to be fired, but criminal charges are also possible.

A lawyer will likely tell you to say nothing: Do not talk to the police or FBI; do not make any public statements or any declaration to your employer. Even though you are innocent, lawyers do not want you to say anything that could put you in prison. This may be good legal strategy. But it is terrible career strategy. Your company will fire you for refusing to explain yourself. The public will assume that you are guilty—otherwise, why didn't you tell your side of the story? Your reputation is ruined, and you will not work again. Your family may even be destroyed under the tremendous pressure. But you may stay out of prison.

I'm not a lawyer, and I can't give you legal advice. You must make the call, but sometimes there are more things you need to protect than the *possibility* of the loss of your freedom. If you are innocent, go ahead and run the small risk of conviction and declare your innocence. Explain the procedures to your employer.

Cooperate with the FBI as you comb the books. Talk to the press and proclaim your innocence. Your lawyers will freak, but their job is to look after only a *segment* of your life. You are the one who must keep all risks in perspective and decide whether avoiding a slight risk of prison is worth the complete destruction of your reputation.

Your career land mine will probably not be as dramatic as the one just described. Thankfully, few of us capture headlines with our troubles, and even fewer have to balance career with prison. But we all face crises, which at the time certainly seem as significant, and the lessons learned from them can also apply here.

7

PLAY THE GAME

My cousin Ralph was hiking through the woods with a friend, Andy. As they were soaking in the nature experience, they turned a corner and came face-to-face with a young bear cub. Ralph was a bit taken aback and did not know what to think, but Andy showed no such hesitation. "Hey, little feller," he said as he picked up the cub. "What are you doing out here all by yourself?" Andy began tossing the cub into the air and playing with him as if he were a puppy. Just as Ralph advised, "I don't think that is a real good idea there, Andy," a roar came from the top of the hill, about a hundred yards away. It was Mama Bear, and she was not happy.

Andy set the bear down and then took off running. Ralph yelled to him, "Andy, you can't outrun that bear!" to which Andy shouted over his shoulder, "I don't have to outrun that bear. I just have to outrun you."

Of course, if you think having to outrun Andy was cold-blooded, realize that it pales compared to having to outrun that coworker who won't hesitate to cut off your legs if it will help him claw his way to the corner office. Sometimes it seems that the pathway to success is crowded with rat-racing politicians.

There are libraries of books dealing with office politics, but they really aren't necessary. Politics is actually a simple subject, and the art can be competently mastered if your head is in the right place.

> Friends may come and go, but enemies accumulate.
>
> —Thomas Jones

If you look upon politics as a grand game and look forward to ripping the guts out of your competition, you're holding the wrong book. (And you will eventually perish in a fiery implosion that cannot be heard over the sound of champagne corks popping.)

But if you see politics as an outgrowth of normal human interaction and something that other people occasionally misuse, we'll cover the subject quite nicely in this one chapter.

Politics is a lot like cholesterol. There is bad cholesterol and there is good cholesterol. But all people think about is the bad member of the group. Well, there are bad politics and good politics. This chapter is going to focus on how to play defense against bad politics and offense using good politics.

Want to know how to play bad politics? You'll have to figure that out on your own. But be warned: people who play bad politics may win in the short term, but it always turns around and bites them in the end. While you will score some early victories and may even see a few promotions, you will leave a trail of enemies who will celebrate your inevitable demise.

> I bring out the worst in my enemies, and that's how I get them to defeat themselves.
>
> —Roy Cohn

Let's look at some solid political strategies, both offensive and defensive. But before we do, let me underscore that every strategy I state is an example of positive politics. In other words, your use of this strategy—whether offensive or defensive—will result in a positive contribution to your company, work environment, and career.

Offensive Political Ploys

This section will not be what you think. I'm not going to teach you how to set up your rival so that he gets fired and you get the promotion. I'm not going to show you how to cut the legs off your boss. That's just not the kind of stuff I want to associate with, and besides, my publisher has made it clear he'd never print such a book.

Just as well, because the things that come to mind when you think of politics really don't work in the long run. When we talk about offensive politics, we are speaking of affirmative actions you can take that will enhance your standing in the company and make other people feel positive toward you. Here are a few successful, positive, offensive ploys.

Take the Blame

Used judiciously, taking the blame for a failure can be a strong way to gain power in an organization. Whoever accepts the blame for a failure eventually gets credit for a project's success.

The trick is to accept blame for a minor setback in the evolution of a project. Others will be quite eager to allow you to do this, since the natural tendency is to separate oneself from blame. But by announcing that you are responsible for the setback, you are also announcing that you are the leader and you are in charge. You then lead the project to a successful conclusion. Since you were so visible when the project had problems, senior executives will also cede you the lion's share of credit for the victory.

Declaring yourself responsible for failure also brands you as a person who accepts responsibility. Look for opportunities to take responsibility; these are most easily found during the darkest days.

You Look Lovely Today, Mrs. Cleaver

You can build a loyal following by making people feel good about themselves. You can do this by paying compliments. You should be liberal in making compliments, but use caution to avoid the perception of brown-nosing. Here is how you can make lots of ally-building compliments without creating the reputation of being a pure suck-up.

Be sincere. Only compliment people when you absolutely believe what you are saying. Don't say "Nice hat" when it looks as though it came out of Carmen Miranda's closet. But when someone impresses you, do not hesitate to make that fact known.

Say good things about your boss to her boss. It is difficult to tell your boss that she did a great job on something without your appearing to be a pathetic yes-man. But if you wait, the opportunity will arise for you to mention it to *her* boss. Now you have scored two points: one with your boss when she hears that you said something nice about her to her boss, and another with the boss's boss, who will note that you are a loyal person to have as a direct report.

Compliment your boss subtly. Actually, it is possible to compliment your boss to his face. Do it in an understated manner. Instead of grinning broadly and shouting, "Great job! Wow, no wonder they put you in charge!" simply look him in the eye and quietly say, "That was impressive. I just learned something there."

Compliment people behind their backs. Use the grapevine for positive communication. When chatting with your target's best friend or close coworker, mention that it looks like Harry has lost a few pounds, or that Martha's report was the best you have read in a long time, or that Sam sure does seem to be catching on to the new training. I guarantee your kind words will get back to them, and no one will accuse you of trying to play up to anyone.

Compliment the act, not the person. "This report is outstanding!" carries much more punch than, "You wrote an outstanding report!" Commenting on the act allows you to go into much more detail and use more superlatives than if you comment about the person directly.

Liberal use of compliments is a powerful, positive political game. But only if you always remember rule #1: Be sincere. An insincere compliment will explode on you and make you look like Eddie Haskell. And that wouldn't be good politics at all.

Recognize Real Power

College students quickly learn that the real power rests with the dean's secretary, not the dean. Learn to recognize influence, not rank. The boss's assistant can get your name on a training list more effectively, let you know the boss's hot priorities, and even let you know when it is a good—or bad—time to approach the boss.

The same situation exists with certain departments in the organization. The humble human resources department may at first glance appear to be filled with meek soldiers, but the fact is that HR people hold enormous direct and indirect control over your career. Although advertised as "support staff," they are often the real power in the organization. Likewise, some major corporations are actually run by the marketing department or the finance department. And we all know that the president's administrative assistant carries far more clout than any department head. Good politics requires you to recognize a person's influence, not his or her rank, and respond accordingly.

Defensive Political Tactics

You probably define *politics* as situations in which other people try to hurt or manipulate you. Since you are kindhearted and focused on the positive, you are just not prepared to fight back when attacked. If you do not possess an evil streak, it would be a serious mistake to play the attacker's game. You don't know how to fight dirty, and so you will fail. Or, as Cousin Ralph reminds me, *When you wrestle a pig, you both get muddy. Only the pig kinda likes it.*

So, instead of playing the adversary's game on her home court, force her to play your game in your stadium. Here are some strategies for dealing with a cutthroat who has targeted you as her next victim.

Let Other People Fight Common Battles

If something unpleasant must be confronted, and it is public knowledge that it is a problem, rest assured someone will volunteer to do battle. Let 'im.

Suppose the receptionist is obnoxious and rude. She's surly and can't do her job right. You know it, and so does everyone else in the building. So should you go to the powers that be and see to it that she gets fired? No, no, no. Let someone else do it.

Suppose management has made a decision about holiday schedules that has the office in an uproar. The decision is universally unpopular and obviously unwise. Be assured many people will volunteer to fight this battle. Your participation is not needed.

If the problem is obvious, someone will take the initiative.

While he will feel some momentary credit, in the long run what will be remembered is that he was the one who raised such a stink and got that poor single mom fired. If you take on the armor of righting every wrong, you will also take on the reputation of being constantly engaged in conflict. Don't fight battles that will soon be fought successfully by others.

Get It in Public

Baseball umpires use a nifty trick when they need to justify throwing out a manager. Umpires are expected to be thick-skinned enough to accept hearing bad language. So a manager's cursing is not enough to justify his being tossed. But umpires are charged with upholding the integrity of the game, so they are considered completely justified in kicking out any manager who uses foul language that can be *heard by the fans*. So, if the umpire has reached his limit, you will notice him slowly creep toward the stands. The manager will unknowingly move along with him, yelling insults about his ancestry, until they are a few feet from the innocent fans. Then the umpire will toss the culprit and explain in his report that he couldn't allow the fans to be exposed to such language.

Follow their lead. Quickly move into a public setting whenever an adversary is behaving in a childish, obscene, or otherwise indefensible manner. Get witnesses. There are many things we can do or say in a more private setting that appear outrageous in public, in front of groups, or even in front of customers.

If an abuser confronts you in your office or some other private setting, follow the umpire's strategy. Slowly walk him or her out the door and into a public setting. (Head to the coffeepot, for example.) The abuser will probably be so engrossed in his tirade that he will pay little attention to his shifting environment, and he'll demonstrate his boorishness to coworkers or customers.

People usually don't get fired for saying *@#**!* in private but are frequently sacked for using foul language in front of a customer.

React Helplessly

My big sister was an airline stewardess in the 1970s. (No, this is not a sexist term. They were called *stewardesses* back then.) She was taught a great trick for dealing with rude, drunk, or otherwise unruly passengers. Start crying. The passenger will look like a heel, and the angry stares from those around will shut him up in a heartbeat.

This trick does not have to be saved for cute, diminutive people. I'm six foot three and weigh (the editor has kindly omitted this number) pounds, but I've used a variation of my sister's technique. I was once in a presentation to some corporate brass when a new member of their group decided to make himself look good by heckling me. I addressed some of his trite observations for a while, but it was getting just plain exhausting. I considered taking him on but recognized that my rank was a peg lower and a direct confrontation might not be wise. (I was perfectly capable of ripping the throat out of his logic and making him look silly but decided that might not be politically prudent in the long run.) So, I decided to give him a rope long enough to hang himself. I let him interrupt several more times, and then I just stopped talking. I shrugged my shoulders, looked helpless, and made eye contact with the EVP. Then I stood back and enjoyed watching the EVP rip the new guy apart for his lack of professionalism and basic ignorance.

> Never keep up with the Joneses. Drag them down to your level. It's cheaper.
>
> —Quentin Crimp

Remember this whenever you are attacked unprofessionally in

a public setting. There will always be a white knight who relishes the battle.

Gotcha

The most frustrating situation to deal with is the person who is respectful and friendly to your face but talks about you behind your back. There is only one successful way to deal with a backstabber, and that is to confront her directly.

When you hear that the backstabber has said something about you, pull her aside immediately. Don't be hostile; just speak to her with an *I-don't-understand* look on your face. Say, "I was just told that you didn't think I was being reasonable in the Hatfield decision. Do you have something you wanted to say to me, or did someone misunderstand your comment?"

> Gossip needn't be false to be evil. There's a lot of truth that shouldn't be passed around.
>
> —Frank Clark

Here's what will happen. The backstabber will deny making the comment, take the "out" you provided, and say it must have been a misunderstanding. She has now learned that you are not afraid to confront her on issues. (This is important because backstabbers fear confrontation. That is why they don't fight their battles directly in the first place.)

Also, the backstabber realizes that the person she initially spoke with will be letting you know whatever is said to him in the future. So the backstabber makes a mental note not to confide in *that* person again, reducing her network by one. Usually, it only takes two or three intercessions like this to get the backstabber off your back.

Backstabbers rarely focus on just one victim. It is in their nature to be this way with all the people they deal with. So the

> It doesn't take a brave dog to bark at the bones of a lion.
>
> —Anonymous

backstabber has a reputation, and there are usually many people who would like to have this stopped. If several victims of the backstabber practice this intervention, you can completely stop this person's behavior inside of a few days.

When Someone Is Picking on You

Remember that unjust criticism is often a disguised compliment. When I was young and would get angry that another child made fun of me, my mom would say, "Oh, he's just jealous." It's true. Sometimes people are so insecure that they criticize others as a way to make their own shortcomings seem smaller.

This is a good time to turn the other cheek. People who behave like children soon develop a reputation, and others see right through them. Although it gets your blood pressure up, their criticisms of you will almost certainly have no effect on your reputation.

Let Him Shoot First

Here is an unwritten rule of conflict resolution: whoever complains first loses. This principle was demonstrated many times in your childhood. Remember getting into squabbles with a playmate who eventually yelled, "I'm going to go tell my mommy!"? Mommy then promptly chastised the kid for being a tattletale and a whiner. Nothing has really changed thirty years later. When someone approaches the boss or the HR department with a personnel complaint, that person is immediately labeled as a troublemaker who is unable to work and play with others.

If you are under an unreasonable attack and your offense is either slight or nonexistent, *encourage* the attacker to take it to the next level. Keep your hands clean, but egg the opponent into complaining. Tell him, "I'm sorry I've upset you. Maybe you should visit HR and tell them what you think." This tactic takes guts and self-assurance, but you will almost always come out of this with the image of being the sober, mature party.

> The trouble with the rat race is that even if you win you are still a rat.
>
> —Lily Tomlin

Take Away the Issue

Gary recounts an embarrassing mistake:

> I often let things slide and put off routine jobs. This sometimes gets me in trouble, but nothing like the time I drove my company car for a year without checking the oil. One day the engine locked up and the company was out $4,000.
>
> This was a pretty big screwup and my non-friends were sure to allude to it whenever they had an opportunity to cut me down a notch. I had to find a way to defuse this hand grenade and found it at a monthly meeting. We were all gathered in the hotel lobby before the meeting began, and there was a commercial on the television. It was about motor oil. To prove the quality of the oil, the commercial showed an engine running for over an hour even after this brand had been drained from the crankcase. The room grew silent and I could see some folks smirking. I paused for a moment, and then quietly said, "Hmmm. Maybe I ought to me get some of that."

Self-deprecating humor removes weapons from your opponents' arsenal. They know that if you are comfortable enough to kid yourself, then their stabbings will not get under your skin.

Destroy Your Enemies

Abraham Lincoln was quite adept at destroying his enemies. He did so by turning them into his friends. Perhaps friendship is too much to hope for, but you can usually turn around how someone treats you by pulling that individual into your camp.

Here's what I mean. Everyone—even the jerk who is hassling you—has strengths. Identify your adversary's biggest strength and ask him for help. That's right, tell him how much you admire a certain skill, tell him that you need his assistance, and pull him in to a critical project you are working on. Everyone likes being asked for advice and assistance. Chances are strong that he will eagerly provide the assistance and begin looking at you in an entirely new light. Most people will respond positively to genuine demonstrations of respect. He'll drop his attack on you because you are now seen as a brilliant person. After all, you were smart enough to recognize his expertise and skill level.

> Never claim as a right what you can ask as a favor.
>
> —John Churton Collins

And Then, *Really* Shovel It On

Now, take this to the next level. When your project succeeds, shower your (former) adversary with praise. Don't be afraid that he'll get the credit. Your boss will give you full credit for any project you head. But your boss will also give you credit for demonstrating outstanding management skills by harnessing the cooperation of someone who was known to be difficult to deal with.

. . . And the Horse You Rode in On

OK, sometimes being nice, responsible, and mature just doesn't solve the problem. At least one time in your career you will be faced with an adversary who is truly out to get you and doesn't respond to the tactics we have discussed.

> You cannot go around and keep score. If you do, you'll find out you are a very miserable person. God gave me the ability to forget, which is one of the greater attributes you have.
>
> —Hubert Humphrey

The fact is, there are some people who are alive only because it is against the law to kill them. While I don't suggest that particular remedy, you do have to make the decision about whether you will take them out or allow them to destroy your career.

How do you fight this war? Sorry, there are just too many scenarios to address. But my point is not to show you how to destroy; it is just to let you know that there are times when you *must* do so. Do not seek out these opportunities, but be perfectly willing to fight when others thrust it upon you. Remember, these folks are not just attacking you; they are harming your livelihood and your family. Don't roll over. Fighting back under these circumstances is not "playing politics." It's basic survival and time for the meek to inherit the earth.

The World's Greatest Political Tactic

Whew. I certainly don't want to end this chapter with those combative words. Instead, let me tell you about the other extreme of politics. This is a political move I learned early in my career, and it has served me well. Heed these words: *Embrace the defeated.*

I learned this lesson from Senator Everett Dirksen, the minority leader of the Senate during the Lyndon Johnson presidency. Whenever there was a vote taking place in which his individual vote would make no difference, he would openly cast his lot with the side that was about to be soundly defeated. According to Dirksen, "The victors never remember and the defeated never forget." He found that later, when he needed to scare up some votes to get a bill passed, he could turn to some of those people he previously voted with on the losing side. They always remembered that he had once bravely stood by them and were eager to repay the kindness.

I once attended a monthly senior management breakfast meeting with the company president. I arrived at the front door to the restaurant at the same time as "Jack." Jack was the VP of finance and had just been notified that he was being terminated at the end of the month. Jack looked at me and said half jokingly, "You'd better wait here a minute. You don't want to be seen walking in with me." I looked him in the eye and said, "I am proud to be seen walking next to you." His eyes teared up, as he felt respected for the first time in the past twenty-four hours. Not surprisingly, Jack remains a loyal business ally today.

Make it a point to befriend the peer who was chewed out at a meeting, or the person who was just forced to resign, or anyone having any type of career difficulty. These people will rise again, your paths will cross, and they will always remember your kindness.

8

MANAGE YOUR BOSS

Baseball manager Earl Weaver was one of the game's finest strategic minds. Reggie Jackson was a perennial all-star and destined to be a member of the Hall of Fame. Reggie knew he was a great player and was also quite impressed with his own abilities to strategize. Conflict between the two was inevitable.

Weaver forbade anyone to steal a base unless he personally gave the go-ahead. Reggie Jackson was not pleased with this rule. Oh, it was understandable for the other players, but Reggie was not any ordinary player. He knew the pitchers and catchers well enough to judge whom he could and could not steal on and took it as a personal insult when someone tried to control him. In one game, he decided to steal without Weaver's approval.

Reggie had no trouble swiping the base. In fact, he got such a good jump that the catcher didn't even bother to make a throw. Jackson smiled as he brushed the dirt off his uniform, knowing he had proven that he was perfectly capable of deciding for himself when to steal a base. He assumed that Weaver's tantrum was just a display of a man who had been shown up.

Weaver later explained why he had not given permission for Reggie to steal. First of all, the next batter was Lee May, who was currently swinging the hottest bat on the team. First base became open when Jackson stole second, so the pitcher walked May intentionally, taking the bat out of his hands. Further, the next batter had never been able to get a hit off the pitcher, so Weaver had to use up a pinch hitter to try to drive in Reggie and May. That wasted bench strength that was desperately needed in later innings. That pinch hitter was not available when a great opportunity arrived in the ninth inning, and the Orioles lost a close game.

> My boss and I have an understanding. He does things his way and I do things his way.
>
> —Anonymous

Now, to understand this chapter, you must understand the point I am *not* making with this story. My point is not "obey your boss because he or she knows more than you and is usually right." Actually, I'm pretty sure that the opposite is true. Most bosses know less about their subordinates' jobs than the jobholders. The sales manager is not the best salesman, for example; it is a completely different job. Microsoft doesn't promote its best programmer to chairman. And the Yankees aren't about to turn Derek Jeter into their third-base coach. Again, different jobs. So my point is not "the boss knows better." In fact, I will cede the argument to Reggie Jackson that he knew far more about being a baseball player than Earl Weaver did.

OK, if that is not my point, what is? Here is why bosses should be obeyed: *The boss is looking after a bigger picture and needs to direct your contribution to that overall strategy.*

Reggie Jackson's job was to steal a base. But Earl Weaver's job was to win the ball game. Sometimes you must do your job differently, not because your boss knows how to do it better, but because he knows what you need to specifically contribute to the bigger picture.

There are times in our careers when we are all Reggie Jacksons. We perceive our bosses' decisions as a bit off base and are certain we could handle decisions far better. Often our analysis is lacking in some of the big picture, and we should defer to the boss's judgment. But there are times when our judgment is credible, and we need to learn how to manage our bosses. However, you cannot be successful unless you understand where your boss is coming from and know his priorities.

This chapter is not designed to teach you how to overpower or overrule your boss. It is designed to show you how to understand his or her needs and work with your boss in a manner that showcases your talents, builds a good team, and gets the boss on your side in promoting your career.

Getting Your Boss on Your Side

Get on the Same Page

Do you sometimes feel that you and your boss are speaking two different languages? You may present some work that you feel is superior, but her reaction is mild. Or perhaps you explain progress on a project, and she has a confused look in her eyes.

What may cause this is that you and your boss have a different understanding of what your job is supposed to do. As off-the-wall as this sounds, there is frequently a disconnect between how you and your boss view your place in the organization. Try this: You and your boss separately make a list of your job responsibilities, objectives, and priorities. Compare lists. You will both be shocked.

> I don't want any yes-men around me. I want everyone to tell me the truth, even if it costs them their jobs.
>
> —Samuel Goldwyn

If you and your boss are working under different assumptions about your role in the organization, is there any mystery about why some of her decisions and reactions appear so alien to you? More important—to you at least—is the terrifying realization that you are being judged on criteria that you are not aware of.

Sit down with your boss and define your job clearly. Have a clear and complete understanding of what she wants you to do and achieve. This simple act of clarity will mend most misunderstandings and cement a much smoother career path for you.

Understand Your Boss's Communication Style

Learn what format, how often, and how thoroughly the boss wants to be communicated with. Observe how he communicates and what styles of messages are most apt to be well received. Does the boss prefer formal memos or quick chats in the hallway?

I had two bosses, back-to-back, with completely opposite communication styles. This can best be illustrated by how I learned to write them memos. The first boss was similar to me. He wanted to know my agenda right up front. You would tell him what you wanted, and if he wanted more information, he would ask for it. So, whenever I sent him a memo, I would state my point in the first sentence; then I would bullet-point my supporting arguments after that. If he agreed with my opening statement, he would approve my request and put the paper aside. If he had questions or needed more information, he would ask.

> If you think your teacher is tough, wait until you get a boss. He doesn't have tenure.
>
> —Bill Gates

My next boss had a different thought process. He was by nature more of an analyst. He wanted to see how I arrived at decisions and felt the process itself was as critical as the conclusion. So with him I would begin a memo by stating the problem, listing several alternative solutions, and then explain how I picked the particular course of action. The last thing in his memo was the first thing in my other boss's memo.

A lot of tension can result when you get the communication styles reversed. If boss A had received memo B, he would have felt I was being tentative and beating around the bush. He would have impatiently waited for me to get to the point, feeling that I was wasting his time because I was feeding him a lot of information he just didn't need.

On the other hand, boss B would be quite jittery receiving memo A. He would consider me rash to begin a memo with a conclusion and would worry that I was trying to put something past him.

Which boss was right? That's just not the point. Your role is not to judge your boss's communication style. It is to understand it. Feed him information exactly the way he wants to eat it. Learning how to communicate with your boss is the biggest strategy you can employ in getting along with him.

Learn Your Boss's Language

Keep in mind that every boss has her own silent expectations. Watch, listen, learn, and add to these when you figure new ones out. Some managers are quite demonstrative, waving their arms and raising their voices at the slightest provocation. For them, an explosion is not something to be concerned about. Other managers are different. My subordinates knew to be extremely worried whenever I began a conversation with "I am disappointed . . ." Something serious was about to be discussed. Learn what your boss means by phrases like "as soon as you can," "if you want to," or "Would you mind . . . ?"

Never Surprise Your Boss

Surprises can be great fun. This is especially true with birthday parties, unexpected visits from relatives, and marriage proposals. But surprising your boss holds no charm and will not bring a smile to his face. Surprises make managers nervous. Bosses and supervisors are expected to know what you're doing, and they get labeled as incompetent by their bosses if they don't know what you are working on. Although there is great drama involved in surprising your boss with a piece of quality work, the pleasure he gets from seeing an unexpected gain is overshadowed by his fear of not knowing what else you are up to.

Another form of surprise is the sin of omission. This is a common mistake young managers make. As an example, let's say you have always hit budget for payroll, but this month you had unexpected problems and used several hundred dollars of overtime. Get the news to her as quickly as possible; never let her first notice be when she reads the P&L statement.

Respond Immediately

Make your boss's requests your first priority. If the boss asks you to do something in the "next couple of weeks" or "when you get a chance," have it on her desk the next day. Seriously. You are making the point that you understand that you work for her and that her needs are your priorities.

> If the boss asks you to do something in the "next couple of weeks" or "when you get a chance," have it on her desk the next day. Seriously.

However, if you do not like that chunk of advice—perhaps you think it is too extreme—then do heed this bit of advice: *never have to be reminded about anything your boss has asked of you.* Beat deadlines and be thorough. If you find that your boss is reminding you of due dates, watch out. She has lost some confidence in you. You probably missed some deadlines or gave her some other reason to worry about you. The only way to cure this is by exceeding her expectations for the next few months and making a point of perfect follow-through.

Keep Him Informed About How Wonderful You Are

Despite all the efforts to the contrary, most managers spend their time dealing with screwups. They focus on problems and react to mistakes. In fact, one of the most-used management styles—management by exception—*only* deals with errors and issues. As a result, routine good work goes unnoticed.

If you are in such a system, you must take overt action to make sure your boss notices your routine successes. Do this subtly and regularly. Get into the habit of sending a one-page weekly memo that states what you have done that week in an unadorned, adjective-scarce manner. List any special problems that presented themselves and how you solved them. She will get the message; she will make ongoing mental notes that you are someone who is taking care of issues and solving them before they hit her desk. (And if she is smart, she will save these memos in your employee file and use them for writing your annual review.) You will develop a reputation for competence and build respect from your boss.

Know When to Leave

One man working for me didn't know when to stop selling. He would come into my office with an idea, usually a very good idea. He would make his point convincingly, and I would usually say yes. And then he would keep talking. He would review the points he had already made and then come up with some new ones, all the while basking in the glory of his easily won victory.

I found this quite tiring and chose to break him of this habit. One day he came in with an idea, and I gave him my usual approval. Then he tossed in more arguments in favor of the plan. I listened for a while and then said, "Now that you say that, Allen, I'll have to change my mind. I think I am going to say no to that idea." It took about three meetings like this before Allen caught on, and he learned a critical lesson in dealing with the boss: *When the boss says yes, shut up and leave the office.*

It Is Easier to Get Forgiveness . . .

I am sure you have heard this advice from someone in every company you have worked for: *Around here, it is easier to get forgiveness than permission.* That clever phrase has led to more posterior mastications than any other advice ever offered. Actually, it may work once per job, but only once and only after you have built a reputation for trust, and then only if the venture is successful.

Until then, run from this cliché. If you develop a reputation for exceeding your authority, you will be labeled hard to manage, and your boss will feel you are uncontrollable. He will constantly worry about what you may be up to, and that is not how you want him to be thinking about you.

If there is a venture you feel strongly about, organize your argument and fight for it. If the answer is no, then move on to something else. Your boss probably knows something you don't.

Managing the Difficult Boss

The previous strategies focus on the everyday things you should do to deal with your boss. But sometimes things are not routine. Some bosses have occasional deficiencies. They can be difficult. Let's look at some of these headache inducers and explore ways to deal with them.

Messenger Killers

There is a senator who was once a leading candidate for his party's nomination for president. While I generally supported his views, I was scared of what would happen if he became president. This is because he had a reputation for a fiery temper. He would absolutely destroy anyone who brought him bad news. His people were terrified of these confrontations. Therefore, they avoided all such contact if at all possible. He was surrounded by yes-men and timid advisors, a formula for disaster for a president.

Your boss must be kept in the loop, and sometimes that means you have to deliver bad news. Some bosses don't take bad news well and shoot the messenger. Regardless, do not run away if your boss is a messenger killer. You must have the courage to do your job and let him know what is happening in the real world. But make certain that you deliver bad news in the right way. There are two essential elements for the proper delivery of bad news:

> Captain, it is I, Ensign Pulver, and I just threw your stinking palm tree overboard. Now, what's all this crud about no movie tonight?
>
> —Closing line from the movie *Mister Roberts*

1. Do it promptly. Bad news ages poorly. As soon as you recognize an issue, bring it to the fore. Don't be panicked about it; never be in a frenzy. Just catch it early when the issue is smaller, and throw some light on it.

2. Spend more time delivering potential solutions than you do delivering news of the disaster. When dealing with your boss, never lay out a problem and then steal away. Always deliver bad

news with a solution in mind. Your remedy may or may not work, but at least your boss knows you are looking to solve the problem, not just dump a mess in his lap. By your doing this, your boss will learn to identify you with solutions rather than disasters.

When the Boss Won't Delegate

There are bosses who tell their people exactly how to do their jobs and make decisions that should be passed down the chain. Consider the complaint of this department manager: "Every decision I'm supposed to make about schedules or sales quotas has to have his approval. It makes me wonder what I'm getting paid for." This is a frustrating existence, and you must address any reluctance to delegate.

Determine what is causing the boss to rein you in so tightly. Perhaps she is not convinced that you are competent. As uncomfortable as this thought is, you must uncover any hidden doubts she has about your abilities. Ask, and be ready to catch any clues she may give by not directly answering your question. For instance, does she change the subject? Pause before answering? Give you ambiguous answers? Probe further if she says things such as, "I'm *generally* pleased . . . ," or "You *usually* deliver what I am looking for." These are indirect ways of letting you know that her failure to delegate is rooted in dissatisfaction with your work.

Address any concerns about your abilities. For instance, if your boss states that he worries that you might not be picking up on holes in purchasing contracts, let him know that you acknowledge this and have enrolled in a business law course to help with your understanding of contract needs.

Of course, a boss's failure to delegate may be more deeply rooted in *his* insecurities than fears of your abilities. You can address this by directly asking, "What can I do to show you that I can handle oversight of training for the sales department?" Let him tell you how to address his fears, and follow through on what he tells you.

Let the boss take baby steps. Get her to assign you small projects, and then deliver them brilliantly. Build her comfort level as you strengthen your reputation as someone who can be entrusted with important assignments.

When You Get a New Boss

The new pastor was meeting with the board of elders for the first time and making a few budget requests. One of them was for $100 a month for mowing the grass around the parsonage. This raised the eyebrow of one elder who commented, "Reverend Charlie always mowed the grass when he was here." The new pastor quickly replied, "Yes, and I checked with him on that, but he just doesn't want to do it anymore."

Getting a new boss is no different from starting a new job. You must begin anew in understanding his priorities, communication style, and goals. Understand that approach and you will quickly establish rapport while the rest of the department is trying to explain to him "the way Charlie always did things around here."

> If you think your boss is stupid, remember you wouldn't have a job if he was any smarter.
>
> —John Gotti

Welcome your new boss, and then give him a week or so to settle in. Then drop by and introduce yourself. Show him the projects you are working on, past results, and an overview of your credentials. And then ask him to tell you what *he* wants done and how *he* wants to do things. Clarify anything you don't immediately understand, and convince him of your cooperation and loyalty. Do not use this time to surprise him with your pet issues or try to get his quick approval on some project your previous boss killed. And do not spread any gossip or offer your opinions on any of your peers. Use this time to gain his confidence, not spark questions about your motives.

Be on Her Team

Learn this concept now: you work for your boss. Your career will not advance if you are perceived as someone always challenging and fighting your boss. You will not get promoted because no one will want you as a subordinate. If you work for someone, then by gosh, work for her. If you can't give her your loyalty and cooperation, then either transfer to another area, wait her out, or find a new job. But until you are able to do this, do everything you can to deliver the results she wants, when she wants, in the format she wants.

Public relations consultant Rex Reed observes:

> Loyalty is the first virtue in my business. Be loyal to your superior and the organization or company. If you ever feel you can't be, either because of the conduct of the company or the superior, or a deterioration in your professional relationship, then move on.
>
> Recently a competitor to an existing client of my consulting firm offered to hire us away from them for a larger fee. I told them politely but gently that we don't build our business by jettisoning friends and clients who helped us grow, even if it did mean more revenue.
>
> So my advice to those who are serving a client or a boss is: be loyal and faithful. Too many people view career opportunities as a chance to make a name for themselves at their boss's expense. A truly successful career is built by helping your boss achieve his or her vision. If you share that vision, then help make it happen. If not, then move on and pursue a different vision.

Those who are successful in "managing up" have a much smoother ride than those who begin each day fearful and perplexed. Those able to manage their bosses know that the process has nothing to do with manipulation, complex psychological analysis, or dirty politics. It is actually a very simple formula. Here is how you successfully manage your boss: Learn what your boss's priorities and goals are and find out how you can best help him attain them.

9

GET PROMOTED

COMPETITION TO BECOME THE HOST FOR *THE TONIGHT Show* heated up when Johnny Carson announced his retirement in 1991. This job was any comedian's dream, and there was no dearth of people lining up for consideration. But despite the campaigns and public posturing by the many candidates, Jay Leno won the job—even before Carson made his announcement. He had it won before all the potential candidates began waving their hands. The job was won even before the NBC executives knew they were going to hire him. It was won because he had executed a promotion plan for several years before Carson's retirement.

Jay Leno knew the day would come when Johnny Carson would retire and television's most prestigious job would open up. He knew he wanted this job and developed a perfect plan to get it. Did he suck up to Carson? No, Carson would not be naming his successor. How about the NBC executives? Surely they were the decision makers. Leno correctly determined that it would not be the executives making the call. The real power in the network was the local affiliates, and they were the target of Leno's campaign.

Leno performed in comedy clubs and was in a different city each week. Knowing that the affiliates were starved for local programming, he would offer to appear on their morning programs whenever he was in town. He was liberal with these favors and did whatever he could to provide for their needs. This personal campaign helped Leno develop close friendships with the station managers and owners in every major market in the country.

> Stephens, I'm giving you a big promotion!
>
> —Larry Tate, Darrin Stephens's boss on *Bewitched*

When the host's position became available, the network executives were leaning heavily toward giving the job to David Letterman. It was well known that even Carson favored Letterman. But the affiliates let it be known that Leno was their choice, and the job was his.

Jay Leno focused on the job he wanted, figured out the best path to accomplish the goal, and tirelessly executed his plan. Letterman and the legion of other candidates never had a chance.

It is true that many promotions occur because a person's talent and skills are noticed. Perhaps the company does a good job of record keeping or succession planning and identifies quality internal candidates when a promotional opportunity becomes available. You may very well get promoted just like that.

But probably not. While it is true that cream rises to the top, so does grease. While you must do a good job and be qualified in order to be promoted, you must also take actions to get noticed and prepare for that new position. That is what we'll examine in this chapter. No gimmicks or silly politics, but helping you to organize an honest strategy to prepare for the next step and to be noticed by the company when that step becomes available. Here are some important parts of any promotional plan.

Planning Your Promotion

Ask for the Job

Cindy was a teacher's aide at a private elementary school that specialized in children with reading disabilities. She had taken this job as an aide when moving into a new area in which regular teaching jobs were scarce.

About halfway through the year, the teacher in her class unexpectedly resigned. This position needed to be filled quickly, and it was an incredible obstacle. Teachers who could fit into the school's special culture were difficult to find even when the administrators had a year to search. The administrators were panicked until Cindy walked into the office with the solution: herself.

Cindy reminded them she was already certified as an elementary teacher, had learned the curriculum, and was completely familiar with the program and its students. And most important, Cindy obviously fit into the culture quite nicely. Official certification in specific teaching methods for dyslexia could be obtained simultaneously with actually doing the job, as most of the teachers at the school had done. The administrators looked at one another with a you-should-have-thought-of-that expression and promoted her immediately.

> As simple as it sounds, the best way to get a promotion is to ask for it.

Many people believe that if they do a good job, they will eventually be promoted. That's just not how things work, however. Your boss probably won't consider you for a new role if you never make your desire for a new position known. As simple as it sounds, the best way to get a promotion is to ask for it.

Follow the Program

Don't reinvent the wheel. Many organizations have established procedures for career progression. Government organizations are a good example. If you are going to have a career in the post office, a government agency, or the military, know that they have established procedures that are clearly spelled out. Learn this bureaucracy thoroughly and use it to your advantage.

Unionized companies will have systems that are heavily skewed toward seniority, even when the position is not covered by a union contract. Investigate this culture before going to work for such a company. Steer clear of these firms if you are uncomfortable with time of service being the greatest criterion for promotion.

Still, most large companies do have organized career-development steps even though they may not be memorialized in any formal program. People in such companies may speak of "having your ticket punched." That means working with different assignments, projects, and departments that will give you the experience necessary for getting the position you seek. Although this ticket punching may be unofficial, it is definable. Work with HR and your supervisor to put some definition to any ticket-punching program at your company.

Make a Plan

You will have to create a career plan if one does not exist. Suppose you want to go from being a credit analyst supervisor to regional credit manager. Ask your boss what kinds of skills, knowledge, and experience it takes to get from point A to point B. Then do everything you can to become the obvious candidate. Take advantage of training programs. Seek out opportunities to shine by taking on key assignments. Network within the field. Keep your boss informed at every step, ensuring that she knows your progress in the very program she helped develop.

Again, get HR involved in your plan. HR people are flattered when they are used for what they believe is their real purpose—developing talent. While most candidates run from HR or view HR people as roadblocks, you can acquire a solid ally by enlisting their help with career planning.

Make It Easy for Them to Promote You

Companies rarely promote someone until they have your replacement ready. Make preparation of a successor an important part of your promotion plan. Clear the way for your own success.

One way to pave the way is to appoint a deputy. Groom your successor by beginning to delegate responsibilities to her. Allow her to perform entire segments of your job, such as monthly forecasting, training, or project management. Gradually stretch the complexity of these assignments as she becomes more comfortable with your responsibilities. In addition to helping her learn the job, this action assures a smooth, rather than abrupt, transition when it does come time for you to go.

Provide regular formal and informal feedback. On a formal basis, shorten the performance review cycle by half. On an informal basis, you could have weekly performance summaries, perhaps combining these discussions with planning for next week's activities.

> Cream always rises to the top. Then again, so does grease.
>
> —Anonymous

You may be unable to identify a single person as your successor. If this is the case, then another strategy is to create a team of prospects and offer all of them mentoring. This may actually be a safer strategy because the company will have more choices when you leave. It will also protect you from losing a promotion because your deputy prematurely quit in order to take a fabulous position with a rival company that you inadvertently developed her for.

Master Your Current Job

As mentioned, your boss's job is not an advanced form of your job. It is a completely different job. So does this mean that you don't need to master your job before being promoted? No.

While your deficiencies in the current job may have nothing to do with the responsibilities of the job you are seeking, the fact is that you will not be promoted to anything unless your current performance is superior to that of your peers. This is not because your tasks must be duplicated. It is because no company wants to promote people who are performing in a mediocre manner. It just doesn't smell right.

Before seeking a promotion, learn your job thoroughly, master the objectives, and perform it in an exemplary manner.

Campaign for the Job

I witnessed a brilliant promotion campaign several years ago. An executive vice president (the number two guy) and one of the regional vice presidents (a notch down the pecking order) were seeking the same job. Both wanted to replace the retiring president of their company. The EVP was an exceptional performer and had a solid reputation in the company. As the heir apparent, he continued with his excellent performance and assumed it was just a matter of time until he was made CEO.

But the regional VP surveyed the situation and put together a great strategy. She spiffed up her professional image, looking like a president rather than a hands-on regional operator. She began taking leadership assignments with her peers. She produced a rousing sales meeting to which she invited the current president and all the board members. She further expanded her relationship with those board members, keeping in touch and finding opportunities to share her insights. Soon, she began to look like the president that the board was seeking. She got the job, and the EVP never saw it coming.

Let Them Take You on a Test Drive

Sometimes the best way to get a new job is to go ahead and do it. Although that might not be completely possible, look for opportunities to demonstrate that you can handle aspects of the position.

For instance, perhaps the new job involves making presentations to management. Ask for opportunities to make such presentations, perhaps filling in for your boss or putting together a recap of a project.

> Movin' on up to the East Side, to a deluxe apartment in the sky.
>
> —Theme to *The Jeffersons*

Or perhaps the new position involves a great deal of budgeting or forecasting. Volunteer to help your boss prepare the annual sales budget, or offer to prepare a portion of the annual forecast, or even do the complete budget for him every other month. Identify the key elements of the job you are seeking. Learn how to do these things, and seek opportunities to publicly demonstrate your competence.

Keep your eye out for opportunities to demonstrate your ability to perform at the next level.

Be Patient . . .

Many people join the church on Sunday and want to be chairman of the deacons Monday afternoon. Lack of patience has doomed more career promotions than lack of competence. A company rarely promotes someone when he feels ready; promotions occur when the *company* is ready. Respect the company's timetable, and accept the fact that your promotion will probably occur sometime after you think it should happen.

A company rarely promotes someone when he feels ready; promotions occur when the company is ready.

Cultivate work relationships with prospective colleagues in the department you hope to join. You are more apt to get the promotion or job-enhancing transfer if the people in the department know you and consider you one of them already. Schedule lunch with members of the department regularly, and seek committee assignments where you will serve with them. Drop by the coffeepot in their department and chat.

Here's a good way to bond with other departments: Go to training classes where its people might also be. For instance, if the company is offering a class in CPR, or PowerPoint, or healthy cooking, go. You'll be sitting alongside lots of people from other departments—of all ranks—and they will see yet one more example of you being "one of them."

... But Not Too Patient

It is quite proper to wait until you are ready, but don't wait until the time is *perfect*. Sometimes you must make your move before all the planets align simply because the opportunity is there. Larry recounts this example:

> I had been a regional director for just six months when one of the division vice presidents unexpectedly resigned. The executive vice president, Paul, announced that he was going to interview every regional director for the position. I had less seniority than all the other directors and was in fact still getting used to my job, so I

assumed this was just a token interview. Besides, I knew it would take me at least another year before I was engrained deeply enough in the company to be a serious candidate.

I used my interview to position myself for the future. I explained to Paul that I realized I was still the new guy and that there were other directors better suited for the promotion right now. I even specifically endorsed one, trying to score some points with a peer. I thought it a brilliant performance, one sure to give my boss's boss a good impression that he would remember in a couple of years when I would be a viable candidate for promotion.

He did select someone else for the job; in fact it was the person I had endorsed. I was feeling good about the whole process until I spoke with Wayne, a friend high up in HR. He dropped a bombshell. It seems that I had actually been the leading candidate for the job, but Paul had been so put off by what he perceived as a lack of ambition that he chose someone else. Wayne gave me some good advice. He said, "Opportunity comes around on its own schedule. You've got to adapt to its timing, not yours."

Let patience be a virtue, not a roadblock.

Get Involved in the Hot Projects or Committees

Seek out the most challenging assignments you can find. Identify the company's priorities, and shape your job to associate with them. Find out what the president's real passion is, and volunteer for the right committees and projects. Be visible also in promoting company causes and charities.

Seek out assignments in which you can do one or more of the following:

- begin a project from scratch
- fix a failing system
- increase the scope of your job
- move from a line position to a staff position, or vice versa

If you want to move up, challenge yourself and put yourself in tough, challenging, stretch assignments. That is where real learning takes place and where people pay attention to your work.

Get Credit

Toot your own horn from time to time. Make your boss aware of any honors you have been given. If a customer congratulates you on doing a great job, ask her to drop your boss a note or an e-mail. Have your boss acknowledge your success in the company newsletter or up on the bulletin board. There are dozens of ways to be recognized for good performance, and you need to be the head of your own PR firm.

Also, make it part of your routine to give your boss a weekly summary of your activities. While the report should be process focused, it only makes sense to include a list of your successes and projects you have accomplished. Your boss will keep these in a file and refer to them when writing your annual performance review.

Ensure a High Performance Rating

Do you think your performance rating system is brutal? Consider how they used to do annual fitness reports in the navy. Before 2001, the commander of each navy ship was required to rank the performance of each officer. There could be no ties. Someone had to be ranked first; someone was ranked last, no matter how capable his performance.

Naval officers take the review process seriously, as should you. This is the only sure thing that hits your employee file;

many judgments are made about you from this annual piece of paper.

Make it easy for your boss to rate you highly. Keep a weekly list of accomplishments throughout the year. A month before it is due, present him with a bullet-point list of accomplishments. If there is a standard format, go ahead and write up your own review of yourself. He will be so relieved not to have to slave over one more review that he may be inclined to use your words virtually verbatim.

Prepare for Meetings

Meetings are opportunities to audition in front of potential bosses. Plan to broadcast a carefully created image. Over a period of time, key players in other departments will create a mental file on you and have you in mind when opportunities occur in their departments.

Carefully prepare for each meeting you attend. Study the list of attendees, and be prepared to include some targeted comments. You can plant seeds that can be harvested for some great career opportunities as positions become available in other parts of the company.

Finally, eagerly volunteer whenever your boss wants someone to sit in for her at an audition—uh, meeting—at which she is scheduled to appear. These are opportunities designed in heaven.

Should You Take the Promotion?

We've dedicated this chapter to the process of getting promoted, but perhaps we should pause for some contemplation. Not every promotion is a positive experience. Let's slow the train's momentum a bit and analyze this promotion before we buy a ticket. Here are some questions to mull over to help guide your thought process.

Is It Really a Promotion?

Seriously, this is sometimes a tough question to answer. If you are a third baseman, is it a promotion to be made the third-base coach? How about moving from salesman to sales manager? Sometimes vice chairman of the board is a prestigious position; often it is the dumping ground for has-beens. Look beyond the title in evaluating promotions. Assure yourself that the position is a logical step in your career progression, that the job has substance, and that it can lead to another positive step.

Does It Fit Your Career Objectives?

Management jobs are usually just that—management jobs. If your career track is sales or architecture or teaching or litigation, being promoted into management may create a career detour. Step back and take a look at the situation. Make sure this promotion actually sends you closer to where you want to be.

I can do that, I said to myself. I was in college, studying to be a graphic artist, and had just seen a job posting. A car wash was going to make a radio commercial, and they were looking for someone who could imitate Mae West. Three days later I cashed a $25 check—my first income as a voiceover actress.

I'd love to report that the offers came pouring in from that day forward, but that's just not the case. After graduation, I was working as a secretary when an executive, who knew I had dabbled in local theatre, asked if I could do a German accent. "*I can do that,*" I said. That led to a radio commercial, which actually won a local award.

Again, I'd love to report that the offers then came pouring in, but that's still not the case. Once I committed to voiceover as a career, opportunities did begin to occur with greater frequency, but I had to maintain other employment while building that career. (Those side-jobs had quite a range to them: a sign painter, telegram singer, the world's worst waitress, secretary, even toiling through a passionate scene in a movie with Antonio Banderas!)

Eventually the voiceover work became a lucrative profession offering much satisfaction and freedom. But it is important to note just how I built that career. It was more than hard work—lots of people work hard. And it really wasn't talent either—the world is filled with quality voices. No, I built a great career by applying a basic business principle: *provide excellent customer service*. I realized early on that I needed to do just one thing. Make the client happy. Period. Here are some ways I put the customers' needs first:

- I never refused work. I knew word would get out that I cared about my clients, so I took every job offered—regardless of how little it paid.
- I kept myself available for the *customer's* schedule. Many people in this business hold second jobs working late into the night. They don't want to be disturbed before noon. But half the jobs are before noon! I was available any time, based purely on the client's needs.
- And I always gave the customer what he wanted. Some people seek to create works of art or win industry awards. I was interested in selling my customer's product.

Soon, word spread that I was versatile and easy to work with. And then, I'm proud to report, the offers *did* come pouring in. Good things happen to your career when you put the customer first.

—Allison Pace
Voiceover Actor
Little Rock, AR

Are You Ready for the New Job?

Companies often have times in which their need for people exceeds their available inventory. The temptation is strong to make a battlefield promotion. While the company's motivation is usually sincere, this action could force you into a position you are not quite ready for. If this is the case, and you stumble in the role, you could set your career back many years.

Be leery of these situations, but don't reject them automatically. The fact is that many people can point to moments in their careers when they stepped up to the plate during a company crisis and took advantage of a great opportunity that would not otherwise be there. You must evaluate the situation as objectively as possible. If you think that there is a strong chance you will fail in the spot and need more time to develop, decline the promotion. If you think that you would be able to get your arms around it, grab the opportunity. Just make sure you evaluate the moment for what it is.

Not Up, but Over

When a promotion is simply not available, consider making a lateral career move. If you like your company's culture, your coworkers, and other intangible qualities of your job, remaining at your company in a different capacity can make a lot of sense. Other positions may offer opportunities to acquire new skills and chances to broaden your experience and networking base. Also, if you've been in the same company for a long time, a lateral move can give you the varied professional experience to round out your résumé.

How to Get a Raise

There is the story of the man who asked for a raise and was refused. So he promptly resigned. When the company began interviewing for his replacement, the man applied for his same job. The company, after realizing how well he stacked up to possible replacements, hired the man back into his old position at a salary even higher than the man had asked for in the first place.

That's a really neat story, but I doubt it ever actually happened. In any event, I don't recommend this strategy. It's just too risky, and real life never plays out as well as these urban legends. (Let's face it: in real life the guy's boss would be angry at him for pulling the stunt and never even consider hiring him back.) You can, however, use this story to support your request for a raise and demonstrate what the company would have to pay on the open market to replace you. Just don't make it sound as though you are threatening to quit if you don't get your way.

Let's return to the real world. Consider this procedure for asking for a raise. Set a meeting with your boss and make the following presentation:

1. Describe all of your accomplishments in the past year. Be specific. Show how your actual results stack up against budget, plans, goals, and so forth. If these accomplishments can be measured in dollars—such as cost savings or incremental profits—so much the better. If they are things that cannot be immediately tagged to cash, find a way to convert them. For instance, decreasing turnover for employees in their first year saved the company $60,000 in training expenses and $112,000 in recruitment expenses. Opening three new stores early allowed the generation of $172,000 of off-plan sales. The point here is to demonstrate numbers that are so large that your salary increase request looks rather minute.

2. Present a list of goals you will achieve in the coming year. This is similar to the previous list but makes the point that your value will continue to generate money for the company in the future.

3. Make your request. After all the big numbers you have been presenting, your compensation increase will seem quite modest.

Therefore, ask for the amount that you actually want, not what you think the company will eventually settle for. The fact is, you will not receive more money than you request; it will almost certainly be a percentage of your initial offer. Make it a large number.

Notice something that you do *not* discuss: do not tell your boss that you need a raise because you can't make ends meet on your present salary. Or that little Amanda needs braces. Or that your good-for-nothing husband just lost his job again. This discussion is never about *your* needs. It is about the company's needs and your ability to solve its problems and make it a lot of money. This discussion will fail if you even mention your needs.

My uncle Fred recently became the head of a research division at a major pharmaceutical company. This was a somewhat unconventional promotion, as his previous job entailed maintaining the building's air-conditioning system. Fred was changing a filter in a room where nine scientists were struggling to cope with the West Nile Virus epidemic, when he made a pretty good suggestion. "Why don't we call the people living in East Nile and find out what they did?" he remarked.

It is possible to be like Uncle Fred and just happen to be at the right place at the right time. Possible, but don't bank on it. You are more likely to be promoted by imitating Jay Leno than my uncle. Make a plan and work the plan, and you will be surprised how often those golden opportunities actually do appear.

Section III

REFINE YOUR CAREER

10

MOVE ON

On his fiftieth birthday, Uncle Larry was taking a long walk through the forest, contemplating the things that fifty-year-old men tend to contemplate. Suddenly, a frog jumped into his path and plopped right in front of him. Larry had to stop quickly to avoid squishing the varmint. He was startled by the frog's boldness, but not nearly as startled as he was by what the frog did next. It spoke.

"Please, sir, listen to me," the frog began in a sexy feminine voice. "I am not really a frog, but a beautiful princess. A wicked witch cast this curse on me. But if you kiss me, I will again become a princess and will serve you forever." The frog then did something that could only be interpreted as a wink.

"Well, I'll be darned," my uncle said as he reached down and carefully picked up the royal amphibian. He then carefully put her in the upper pocket of his jacket and resumed his walk.

"What are you doing?" cried the frog. "Didn't you hear me tell you that I would become a beautiful princess if you kissed me?"

"Yes, I did," my uncle replied. "But at this point in my life, I think I would rather have a talking frog."

We all have times in our lives when our priorities change. Hitting an age ending in zero, children out of college, reaching the top of our profession—these are all landmarks where we reevaluate our lives and our future. We seek a new direction; and that new direction often means changing careers.

But sometimes this decision is made for us. Layoffs, restructuring, and outright terminations will push us into the marketplace when we don't want to be there.

Whether the decision is voluntary or thrust upon us, changing jobs is a process that is usually dreaded, at best. This explains why so few people use it as a proactive tool in building their careers and instead only change jobs when the process is forced upon them.

Your reason for looking for a new job has a dramatic effect on your career progression. Simply put, your career will not progress well if the only time you look for a job is when you are unemployed and in desperate need of one. The best time to leave a job is when you are on top and are under no pressure to look for something else. While later chapters will help you work through situations where you are forced to seek new employment, this chapter focuses on changing jobs on your own initiative.

There are several reasons you may begin to look for new employment while still healthily employed. You may have been passed over for promotion one time too many and realize that this company will not meet your career needs. Your boss or mentor has left the company, and no one has equity in you any longer. Your company's reputation is slowly fading, and you fear its long-term effect on your résumé. A new industry catches your eye, or, like Uncle Larry, you are at a time in your life when you just need an adjustment. Let's study that scenario in a bit more detail.

Job Burnout

Tasks that you used to pursue with glee are now looked upon with contempt. You circle the block a few times before parking your car and walking into your office. You always seem to feel tired, can't think clearly, and probably can't get a good night's sleep. What's going on? These are symptoms of a common career problem, job burnout.

Job burnout is essentially job depression. And the fact is that you cannot leave this depression at the office. It will affect everything in your life, business and personal. When your job goes bad, your life gets rotten. It poisons relationships, assassinates your health, and saps your ambition.

> We all have big changes in our lives that are more or less a second chance.
>
> —Harrison Ford

Everyone hits this wall at one time or another in a career. It usually is a short stage in your life, passing in a week or so. If it continues to linger, or if this depression repeats itself regularly, then you have a serious problem that must be addressed. One of the problems of job burnout is that it affects your entire psychological well-being, not just your career. Many people wrap their entire self-worth in their jobs, so there is nothing left if the job goes bad.

An important way to deal with burnout is prevention. Create a more balanced life beforehand. Have other factors in your life that provide satisfaction—family, recreation, volunteer work, hobbies. Different interests will provide several sources for satisfaction and accomplishment. Not only will this help you cope with the effects of job burnout, it will probably also help prevent that burnout. Keep your life in balance. You will be more productive when you take time for vacation, family, and hobbies.

But once burnout strikes, you have to deal with it. A critical thing to address is making certain that it is your job you are dissatisfied with. Family issues, health problems, and the infamous midlife crisis will all lead to depression, yet the first thing most people want to blame is the job. Don't try to solve your depression by self-diagnosing your villain as your career. In fact, don't do any self-diagnosis at all. Do you think you are a victim of burnout? See a professional, and ensure that your issue isn't clinical depression. Depression is a lot cheaper to treat than changing careers.

Most feelings of being burned out are temporary. We all have times when we are exhausted or just plain fed up with our work. These speed bumps can be dealt with by taking a long vacation, focusing on our families, or just waiting things out. Do not mistake these inevitable aggravations as evidence of a permanent burnout. Try to look deeply at your job and remember when there was magic in it. Find ways to rekindle that magic and rediscover what led you down that path to start with.

Sally Meineke is a retail operations specialist. She observes that there are some definite times you need to consider moving on:

> When you stop enjoying your job—it's time to move on. If you aren't happy in a job, others know it, including your boss. My own experiences have proven one thing to me: When one door closes another opens to an even better opportunity. Never let worry take over your life. It's a waste of time and spirit.

Take some time; you need to assure yourself that this particular career path has come to an end. If you do indeed have burnout, then you have only one satisfactory option: You must seek a fork in the road and travel down it.

Changing Careers

Adults are constantly asking their children what they want to be when they grow up. The reason they do this is that they are looking for suggestions. According to a *Wall Street Journal* poll, half of all Americans want to change careers. Most do not ever attempt to do this, and for good reason. It is about five times as difficult to find a job in a new profession as to get one in the same industry. That is a mountain most people will not attempt, and they are destined to spend the rest of their lives treading water in an ocean of melancholy.

For the small minority who do take on the challenge, they will find the experience perhaps the most exciting and satisfying project of their lives. Changing your career is quite possible as long as you plan the change and execute it intelligently.

This major life change should never be done on a whim. Actually, it *cannot* be done on a whim; poor planning and thought will doom such a move to failure. Here are some critical things to consider before making such a change in your life:

Are You Sure?

Now, here is a basic question that most people decide with their immediate gut feelings. But you must take care that your negativity toward your profession is truly directed at that profession and not just a scapegoat for other life problems. Yes, you may be miserable, but are you sure it is your job that is making you unhappy? We sometimes take out our emotions on the wrong person or thing. Never change careers on short notice.

You must be sure that you are leaping into a new profession, not just escaping from an old one. You are doomed to failure if your career change is solely motivated by a desire to get out of a job. Your motives must be positive, not escapist.

Explore the New Profession

Nothing is worse than leaping before you look. Make sure you're not escaping into a field that fits you just as poorly as your last one. Read about the industry and talk to people who currently work in it. Confirm that your talents and interests are a match for the new field and that you would be happy.

Danger sign: If you cannot find anything unappealing about the job, you almost certainly don't know enough about it.

Your best way to learn about the profession is to talk with people currently in it. Develop contacts in the new profession and make sure you have a solid support system within the industry. Recruit a mentor and join professional associations. Use the Network Referral System that we will describe in Chapter 11.

Make certain that you know the drawbacks and you are able to accept them. Danger sign: If you cannot find anything unappealing about the job, you almost certainly don't know enough about it. All professions have drawbacks. If you don't see any, then you have not explored the field sufficiently.

Also, consider working part-time or volunteering. You will learn about the field and can make key connections for when you're ready to take the plunge.

Seek Lots of Advice, but Make the Decision Yourself

Never abdicate this decision to a career counselor or a career-transitions agency, expecting that they can tell you which field to enter. Career advisors are facilitators; they will follow your lead. They can help explore your interests and discover hidden talents, but you should do the research and make decisions yourself. Anyone who offers to tell you what to do is dangerous.

Never Be Seduced by Hot Industries

Remember the family friend who whispered "plastics" into Dustin Hoffman's ear in *The Graduate*? Actually, that truly was a great industry to get into in 1966. But it was lousy advice for Hoffman personally, and it didn't fit him whatsoever. We've gone through plastics, dot-coms, and investment schemes, which were dynamic industries at the time. But just because they are hot does not mean they are for you. When you enter a field just because it's hot, burnout isn't far behind.

Ensure You Have the Skill or Education

Do you need more education or training? If more training would help you get into your new industry, consider classes at a community college, correspondence courses sponsored by most universities, or a training program offered over the Internet. There are many educational opportunities available, many of which can fit into your schedule while you are still doing your old job. Some industries are so eager for new talent that they will train you in your new field.

Don't Let Money Pull You in or Run You Off

There's not enough money in the world to make you happy if your job doesn't suit you. Workplace dissatisfaction and stress is the number one health problem for working adults. This is particularly true for career changers, who initially earn less at the beginning of new careers. On the other hand, be realistic. Your new job must be able to support the lifestyle you and your family require. So, even if the job fulfills all your hopes and dreams, scuttle it (or supplement it) if you can't pay the bills. I want you to be happy, but don't be a fool about it.

Be Realistic

You are fantasizing if you think your dream job will be the antidote to all your troubles. Know that a new profession will give you a fresh outlook on life and satisfy many of your personal needs. But it in itself will not save your marriage, cure depression, or make women swoon at the mention of your name. Make sure you are doing this for the right reasons, and expect realistic effects on your life.

Secure the Support of Your Family

You will not make a successful career change without it. There are few absolutes in this world, but this is one.

Leap Self-Made Hurdles

Changing careers at midlife can be scary. There is so much to consider and so many obstacles to hurdle. You must take these hurdles into consideration before making the leap. However, while it is prudent to evaluate reasonable roadblocks, do not clutter your thinking with negative myths and unreasonable thoughts. For instance, look at some common myths that will poison your thought process.

I'm too old to make a career change. The most oft-quoted advice from Dear Abby (or was it Ann Landers?) had to do with someone trying to decide whether she should go back to school and get her college degree. "It'll take me five years and I'll be fifty-one by then," the despondent reader noted. Abby replied, "And how old will you be in five years if you don't go back to college?"

That bit of advice has become a cliché specifically because of its truth. There are lots of good reasons not to make a change in careers, but don't you dare let age stand in your way. You can change careers at any age. Ask Colonel Sanders, Grandma Moses, Tom Clancy, and James Michener.

I just don't want to start over at the bottom. You probably won't have to. Starting at the bottom is reserved for those people who have no experience at anything. But you already understand good work habits, office routine, and how to deal with people. You also have sizable knowledge in the field you are leaving, and you will be surprised how much of your business knowledge is directly transferable to your new career.

The key to bypassing entry-level status is to focus on these learned skills during the interview process. The things that made you successful in a job you disliked will probably propel you to success in a field that motivates you. Convince yourself of these skills and you will also be able to convince the person who interviews you. This will set you apart from your younger competition and help you leapfrog some of the entry-level assignments typically associated with changing industries.

I can't change industries; I don't have any inside connections. True, it is easier to get *any* job if you know someone working for the company. And it does help to know people in high places. But you don't have to have a network in place to break into something new. You can create that network, usually by extending the people in your current network. (We explore how to do this in Chapter 11.) Changing industries or professions is certainly more difficult than staying where you are. You should not take this challenge for granted, but neither should you build it into an obstacle of mythical proportions.

Headhunters, Recruiters, and Search Firms

Since the next chapter explores how to find a job, you would think that this section would be placed there. But it is intentionally placed here for a critical reason: *Headhunters are of tremendous value to you when you are not looking for a job. They are darn near useless when you are unemployed.*

Long-term career development, headhunter good. Urgent need, headhunter nearly useless. Let me explain why.

A professional headhunter is employed by a company to find an executive who will fit a narrowly defined job and will fit into a certain niche. Most recruiters are engaged in just a few searches at

> All change is not growth, as all movement is not forward.
>
> —Ellen Glasgow

any one time. The chances of a headhunter working on a specific search that fits you at the exact time you need a job are quite slim.

I shake my head when I call someone about an excellent opportunity and hear this response: "That job sounds fantastic, but I'm not really looking right now." Headhunters are a source of tremendous career opportunities. To cash in on these opportunities, you must adjust your timetable. Frankly, what makes you attractive is the very fact that you are *not* looking. Clients are not impressed with a headhunter who brings them a candidate who is currently unemployed. I know many headhunters who will not even present an unemployed person, believing the client will think he didn't have to work very hard to find her.

So many times I have been rebuffed by a potential candidate, only to receive a desperate call a month later. There is not much I can do at that point because nothing lowers your stock value like desperation.

Most people think that recruiters and search firms are sitting on a huge stack of available jobs and that when they call them, the headhunter will eagerly match them up with several opportunities. People get frustrated because the same headhunter who was continually knocking at their door a year ago shows little interest today.

To properly use a headhunter, you must understand this fact: the great next step in your career is rarely available at the exact time you are seeking new employment. Opportunity knocks at its own schedule, and you have to adjust your timetable to fit it.

But how do you build a relationship with a headhunter so that he knows to call you when something does become available? I recommend you not be coy about this. Identify three or four executive recruiters in your industry, and approach them directly. Tell each one that you are solidly employed, seem to be on the fast track, and have no plans to move. But you know the realities of the corporate world and want him to be aware of you and your career should anything exciting come to his attention in the future. Send him your résumé and keep in touch, adding that headhunter as a valuable member of your network. Periodically send him articles you have published, kudos in the company newsletter, or any interesting (nonproprietary) information you have learned.

Most of all, do the headhunter favors. The biggest favor is to respond quickly whenever he asks you for the names of possible candidates for positions he is filling. His asking you for referrals is a sign that you are in his trusted network; providing them is the very best way for you to establish a close relationship with a headhunter.

Should You Go to the Interview?

Some job seekers actually struggle over whether or not they should interview for a job a headhunter passes in front of their noses. Frequently, they perceive that the job is at too low a level, or the company just doesn't excite them. I contend that you should go on *every* interview you can. There are many reasons to do so. Here are a few:

- You may discover that there is much more to the job than first met your eye and that the opportunity actually does excite you.
- You may discover that the company has a lot more going for it than you thought. For instance, it may be on the verge of a new technology, or the boss is someone who is particularly dynamic, or the word on the street is just plain wrong.

- The job you interview for may be all wrong for you, but the company may have something better suited that has just opened up.
- You will dramatically improve your network. The interviewers might have a friend who has a job that will be perfect for you.
- The job that was advertised is being revised, and you happen to be a good fit for it.
- What's the worst that can happen? You improve your interviewing skills, enhance your self-confidence, and maybe get a free lunch.

I have gone into some detail on this for a reason. Refusing to go on interviews is just about the biggest mistake I see job seekers make. You never know about a job until you explore it in some detail. Refusing to interview makes as much sense as refusing to date someone unless you are fairly certain that you will marry her.

But Whatever Happened to *Loyalty*?

Your best opportunity for finding a new, better job comes while you are still employed. Some people will see this strategy as being disloyal to their company, the corporate equivalent of cheating on their spouses. We need to discuss this concept of loyalty because misinterpretation will lead to undue stress and the missing of many career opportunities.

Loyalty to your spouse and loyalty to your company are two completely different concepts. For one thing, no one takes a vow before God to stay with a company "till death do us part." (And unless you are a federal judge, your company would never consider offering you lifetime employment either.) That is just not the nature of the relationship, no matter how loyal the employee or compassionate the company.

So what is your responsibility to be loyal to your company? Loyalty means that you deliver the very best work product you possibly can while you are employed by the company. It is as simple as that. If you have given your best efforts during the time the company has provided you with a paycheck, the ledger is both legally and morally balanced. You seek other employment and other opportunities with a clean conscience as long as you continue to provide your best efforts and do not divulge any company secrets in the process.

> Refusing to interview makes as much sense as refusing to date someone unless you are fairly certain that you will marry her.

Kent recounts this experience:

> I passed up a terrific career opportunity early in my career just because of this concept of loyalty. I was the director of operations for a small chain of retail stores that was experiencing some tough times. We didn't even know if we could keep the company running for another six months, and the stress was enormous. During the peak of the crisis, I was approached by a large (stable) company for a significantly higher position and a large pay increase. In fact, at this point in my career, this would be an impressive, career-making situation. Unfortunately, I was twenty-four years old and carried all the idealism that age offered. I declined the job because "my people need me to lead them through these tough times." (Ugh. Talk about an oversized ego.) Think about that. I jettisoned my obligations to my family and ignored my responsibility for my own career development because I thought I owed it to my current employer.
>
> The results? Within a year, most of those people who "needed me" had left for more stable jobs. So had my boss. But my company survived, by wisely reorganizing operations, which saved it

enough money to keep it afloat until they were bought out by a competitor. Unfortunately, a key element of that money-saving reorganization was to lay me off.

How to Leave a Job Properly

When you part company, *how* you leave may be just as important as any single thing you have accomplished while working for that company. Your behavior during departure creates a lasting memory for management and coworkers. It says much about your professional character and personal integrity. Quash the urge to gloat when you resign. Leave on good terms with as many people as possible. The world is too small for you to tell the annoying coworker just how much you won't miss her, and it will only hurt you in the long run to tell the boss that he's a boor.

Offer reasonable notice. Two weeks to a month is the norm. Never leave it open-ended. ("I'll stay until you hire and train my replacement.") Don't be coerced into staying longer. Notice is a courtesy and should not be taken advantage of.

Keep explanations simple. I had an acquaintance who absolutely despised her boss, her job, and her company. However, they thought well of her and had no clue as to her level of spite. That was until the day she took a similar position with her company's greatest competitor. She used the occasion to write a scathing resignation letter, listing all of her boss's incompetencies as well as the company's monumental shortcomings. She felt good getting this off her chest and smirked through her tenure with her new company. Which, incidentally, came to an undig-

> Writing a resignation letter is the only time in which it is ethical to absolutely lie through your teeth.

nified end just hours after her original employer acquired her new company.

If you decide to resign, it was for "better opportunities." That's it. A resignation letter should simply state you are leaving and when. Add a note, no matter how insincere, that you appreciate your tenure, learned a lot, and will miss everyone. Writing a resignation letter is the only time in which it is ethical to absolutely lie through your teeth.

Counteroffers

Do not be surprised if your employer presents you with a counteroffer when you resign. I am going to spend some time on this subject because mishandling a counteroffer can absolutely derail your career.

A counteroffer is an attempt by your employer to keep you after you have tendered your resignation. It usually represents a variety of new commitments, such as an overdue promotion or a bigger salary, greater benefits, a reduction in hours, less overnight travel, or an offer of other rewards. But it represents something far greater than the sum of its financial benefits. To many people it represents vindication, attention, and overdue appreciation. Or, in the words of Sally Field upon accepting the 1984 Best Actress Oscar, "*You like me! You really like me!*"

Heed these words: all accepted counteroffers end in disaster. If you accept your employer's counteroffer, you will be looking for another job within six months.

Understand why this is. Companies are often shocked when an employee resigns. They may even take it as a personal rejection and decide to try and keep you in order to save face. They will offer to top the salary, commit to training, or even promise you a promotion. This counteroffer must be taken for what it is—a shocked reaction to personal rejection.

Starting a New Job

Even as teenagers, we knew the power of a first impression. We learned this when dating, as we spent hours picking the right clothes, applying perfect makeup, or shining up Dad's car before meeting a blind date.

Many people forget this lesson when starting a new job. Just like the moment your date opens the door and catches the first glimpse of you, just like a job interview when the interviewer makes his decision right after the initial handshake, your first few days on the job will pretty well generate your image during your tenure with that company. Yes, you can trace a great deal of your image, power, and success in your new company to how you introduced yourself to that company.

> When you are through changing, you are through.
>
> —Bruce Barton

Wow. That is a bit overwhelming to recognize, and you probably want to challenge the statement. OK, ponder this: Think about three or four of your coworkers. How much different is your perception of them today from your perception during the first few days they came to work at your company? There may be some exceptions, but for the most part you probably perceive them now the same way you did after the first week. The same goes for you: you will be perceived in the future as you were perceived from the start. For this reason, as well as maintaining your sanity as best you can, it is a good idea to have the best possible start to your new job.

Remember that you are the new person coming into a situation where relationships have already been formed. You are the only one who can't find the restroom, doesn't know where the paperclips and stamps are hidden, doesn't yet realize that the receptionist holds all the real power, and doesn't know not to talk to the boss until she's had her first cup of coffee. You have to learn the culture, the product, and your job before you change the world. Your initial few weeks will set the pace for your entire tenure with this new company. Let's study some of the key factors in getting off to the right start.

Before You Ever Clock In

Get to know as much as you can about your new company before you begin your first day. Learn about the product lines, the philosophies, and the corporate culture. Begin by getting information on the very day you accept your new position. Ask for operations manuals, newsletters, and recent memos. Get the password to the intraoffice Web. Take the time you have off to do some research.

Study the company's products. If it includes household consumables, fill your pantry with its detergent, ketchup, furniture polish, or whatever. Dine in its restaurants. Read its magazines. Become an expert consumer of your new company's products.

Study your company's Web site, and learn how it presents itself to the public. You may also be able to find an employee guerilla site in which the employees post their gripes and grievances. Though you don't want to start your tenure off in a negative mind-set, it is useful to see what the recurring themes are and know which employees you need to avoid (more on this later).

Call around to see if anyone in your network knows any of your future coworkers, and ask that person to introduce you prior to your start day. Wouldn't it be nice to see a friendly face when you first walk through the door?

You will think of other ways to learn about your company before your actual start date. The point is that the more you know, the easier you will find the transition.

Walking Through the Door

In an ideal orientation, you will walk into your new job, and your boss will be there to greet you. He'll explain his expectations and hand you a well-organized folder describing your first assignment. The HR representative will take you for a delicious lunch, where you will be introduced to all your new peers at a surprise party they throw for you. Then you'll return to the HR office, where all your benefits are explained to you and all the necessary employment forms are ready for your signature. Then, after a refreshing nap, you will go to your new office, where all the equipment and supplies have been carefully laid out for you. You will pick up the assignment folder and attack your first project with gusto.

Your first day on the job will probably not go quite like this. It is not that your new employer is hostile or even disorganized. It's just that most employers really don't think through ways to make the first day productive, so it is up to you to take charge of the orientation.

Make arrangements to be introduced to the key people in the organization. Be bold. Even if you are the assistant supply room clerk, no company president will refuse a ten-minute introductory meeting. Arrange as many meetings as you can for the first week, and treat these meetings as you would job interviews. You have the chance to orchestrate the only first impression you will ever have with these key people, and that impression will be a lasting one.

Of course, the first meeting you must arrange is with your new boss. Review your job description and ask her if there is anything important not listed. Have her rank your responsibilities for importance. Very often, roles are not cast in stone. The reason you have inherited a particular job specification may be simply that your predecessor chose to work this way. Find out how much flexibility your boss allows and how she would like to see your position evolve. Review current projects, get deadlines, and again, determine importance.

This is an excellent time to examine your annual review form. Have your boss go over exactly how you will be measured and evaluated. Doing this not only crystallizes your new job for you, but it is a great exercise for your boss. She will better establish in her own mind her expectations for you; this exercise helps start you off on the same page.

Be Like a Wolf

When introduced to peers, make it clear to them that you know you have a lot to learn. People are often leery of the new guy, looking for signs that he's a know-it-all or that he thinks he is better than the others. Study wolves. When joining a new pack, they roll over on their backs and expose their necks to prove they are submissive. (Never mind that they intend to later rip the guts from the dominant male. They want to be under the radar initially.)

You should adopt the new wolf's strategy and prove you want to fit in with the team. Ask intelligent questions. Get opinions from your peers and show respect for their hard-earned practical education. Make it clear that you want to be one of them. This introduction will ensure that your new peers wrap their arms around you as one of the team rather than stand back and manufacture defenses against the stranger who just rode into town.

Eagles and Pigeons

Pick your group immediately. Every company has the disgruntled workers who immediately pounce on the new workers. They immediately spew poison, complain about the boss, and want to teach the new guy about "how screwed up things are around here." Run quickly from these people. Do not get sucked into their coven. You will be labeled by management as well as your peers as being infected, and you will be forever ostracized.

On the other hand, there are "gruntled" team players, gilt in gold. They are positive, friendly, and on the fast track. Associating with these people will bring you success and peace. I exaggerate only a bit. The fact is that your image with the new company will be forever labeled based on who you initially associate with. Both the poison apples and the golden "gruntleds" are easy to identify. Make your selection immediately.

Never Say These Words

Every company and office has its way of doing things. This routine may be efficient, or it may be a Rube Goldberg machine. You will not understand the new system for a while, and instant analysis is foolish. Do not change anything until you understand how things currently work, how they got to be that way, and why they got to be that way.

> Never utter these words: "That's not how we did it at my old company."

While one of the reasons you were hired is the experience you bring to the table, you must remember that every workplace has its own way of doing things. Your first few weeks or even months on a job are not the time to change the way things get done.

There will come a time when it will be proper to make some changes. But until that time comes . . . and actually even when that time comes . . . never utter these words: "That's not how we did it at my old company." These words will only generate resistance, hostility, and at least one person replying, "If things were so good at that place, why didn't you just stay there?"

Take Responsibility for Solving Problems

Don't wait for the company to "assimilate" you. Don't wait to be given work to do. It's up to you to establish yourself as a valuable employee as quickly as possible. Jump in and start doing the job.

> If we don't change, we don't grow. If we don't grow, we aren't really living.
>
> —Gail Sheehy

Here is a strategy for starting off right: Seek an assignment that will give you an early win. It could be cleaning out the stockroom, recruiting a dynamic salesman, settling a nagging lawsuit, or fixing a leaky faucet. It doesn't matter how significant the problem is in the scheme of things; what matters is how visible it may have been. Get this early win and you will immediately gain a reputation for competence and contribution. One important point on choosing this project, however: never fix something that puts down a current employee. For example, choose a problem caused by your predecessor, not a current boss.

It is indeed rare to find anyone today who still lives in his birthplace, performing the same job for the same company for the past forty years, while married to the same spouse. Change is inevitable and we must embrace it.

How we handle change determines our career success as well as our personal contentment. Anticipate several major career and personal changes during your life. Learn how to use this change to strengthen your career and grow as a person.

11

FIND NEW OPPORTUNITIES

RIGHT AFTER THE GREAT DROUGHT OF 1989 CAME THE Great Flood of 1990. (Things do tend to rotate that way in the South.) It was then that Uncle Daniel, who had recently returned from a revival meeting, was given an opportunity to test his faith.

Dan refused to evacuate when the waters rose around his house. As the floods approached, a neighbor invited him to jump on the back of his motorcycle. Dan refused, saying only that the Lord would take care of him. When the water covered the first floor of his house, a ranger came by in a boat and begged him to come through the second-floor window and ride the canoe to safety. Again, Dan refused, knowing the Lord would save him. Later, while Dan was trapped on the roof, a helicopter hovered overhead, trying to rescue my uncle. Again, he waved it off, declaring that the Lord would save him.

Finally, Dan was on his tiptoes when he shouted to the heavens, "Lord, why have You not saved me?" A voice boomed from the clouds: "What do you want? I sent you a motorcycle, a canoe, and a chopper."

There are many tools at our disposal when the time comes to find a new job. Sometimes we may even expect to be whisked into a new situation with relative ease, such as seeing the ideal job in the local paper. While they require considerably more effort, other sources can make your job search quicker and much more effective. Let's look at all these lifeboats. We'll begin with the traditional sources that people first think of when they need new employment; then we'll move to those that are much more effective but require substantial effort.

The Traditional Job Market

About 20 percent of the available jobs can be found through traditional sources. These include newspaper classified advertising, Internet job postings, and headhunters/search firms. We'll discuss the sources for the other 80 percent later in this chapter, but first let's examine the first places people think of to look for a job. This is referred to as the *traditional job market.*

Online Job Sites

Online job boards, such as headhunter.net and monster.com, appear to be the solution to your job-search needs. *Wow*, you think. *I can place my résumé on the Internet, and every employer in the world will read it and evaluate it.* Surely, you conclude, this will lead to a stampede to your front door.

You post your résumé and wait. Two days later, you discover that your e-mail box is full. Yippee! You start to read and wade through a long line of advertisements for diet secrets, multilevel marketing opportunities, mortgage refinancing, and exotic vacation timeshares. But no job offers. What happened?

Do not be shocked or discouraged. It isn't you; it's the medium. The whole premise is wrong. On a typical day, a major job board will receive more than thirty thousand new résumé postings. Add this to the half million or so already online. How can a company plow through this massive stack of electronic

> When written in Chinese, the word *crisis* is composed of two characters. One represents danger and the other opportunity.
>
> —John Kennedy

paper and find your specific résumé? It can't.

Does this mean you should ignore this medium? No. Even a blind squirrel occasionally finds a nut. But do not put a lot of hope on this method finding you a great job.

There is a more active way to use the Internet in your search. Rather than posting your résumé, you can prowl the help-wanted ads placed by employers and headhunters. There are often excellent opportunities here that you will not find in the newspaper. That is because the Internet is much more cost-efficient than the daily paper, including a plethora of Web sites in which job postings are free.

You would think that you could find the best jobs on the expensive paid sites, but you would be amazed at the quality and quantity of jobs available on government-sponsored sites.

Since few job hunters are aware of these boards, you will have less competition than on the name-brand sites that advertise on the Super Bowl. Perhaps the best of these sites is *America's Job Bank*. It can be viewed at www.ajb.org. You will find extensive listings here, including most jobs offered by federal, state, and local governments. Your local or state labor departments will know of other similar sites, usually focused on your area.

Newspaper Classified Advertising

Newspaper classifieds are the first place most people look when job hunting. It is also the least effective method for finding a new job. Why the disconnect? Because there is no easier method: A job is posted, I send a résumé, and they hire me. Perfect.

But not exactly. A typical ad in a major-market newspaper receives a thousand responses. That is a tall stack of paper for the HR person to plow through, and you have a huge number of competitors. The odds you'll get that job are pretty slim.

But there are ways you can improve them. Here are some ideas for making the most effective use of newspaper classified advertisements.

The girls all get prettier 'round closing time. When you send in your résumé often has a great deal to do with your chances for being interviewed. There are two reasons for this.

First of all, one of the reasons classified ads attract so many responses is that many job seekers believe it is effective to shotgun their résumés to every ad they see. About half of the responses I receive for positions I post come from people who are in no way qualified for the position advertised. I generally receive these inquiries within just a few days of posting.

If you apply to an ad immediately, your excellent résumé and cover letter get stuck in the same bag as all these others. The screener will not have more than a few seconds to scan your credentials. Because of this, I put a different twist on the postal slogan: Avoid the rush; mail *late*. Your on-target résumé will arrive as the mass postal avalanche from the rabble begins to trickle, and your credentials will be given the time for analysis they deserve.

> Opportunities can drop in your lap . . . if you place your lap where opportunities tend to drop.
>
> —Anonymous

Also, companies have great expectations when they post an ad on the Internet or in the newspaper. They believe that if they post it, they will come. The ad appears in the paper, and the résumés immediately begin to flood in. These are eagerly perused. Candidates who are not a perfect fit are immediately tossed, usually with a sneer and a comment like, "How dare they pollute us with their inferior credentials." After a few days and a few hundred résumés discarded, though, the company begins to realize that there will be no perfect candidate. No one will have all the required credentials. The hiring managers are discouraged and fear they'll never find who they want.

Then *you* miraculously show up as the answer to their problems. After the first week, the standards settle to a more realistic level, and they'll even ignore the fact that you are missing a qualification or two. Wait about a week to ten days and you have a better chance of being evaluated more favorably.

A good rule of thumb is to apply if you meet 80 percent of the listed requirements and if your knowledge of the position tells you that you can do the job with the credentials you have.

Should I even apply? Sometimes an advertisement lists credentials that you don't have. They may be asking for a master's degree for an entry-level job, or excessive years of experience, or even certifications that just don't match the position. You see these extreme "qualifications" and figure you shouldn't even bother to apply.

Think twice before doing this. Are the requirements really required to do the job? Sometimes people writing the ads merely put together a wish list, often exaggerating their real needs. Does the job really require an MBA? If not, go ahead and apply with your BBA. Does it really require ten years of experience? If you have six and know you can do the job, go ahead and submit your résumé.

A good rule of thumb is to apply if you meet 80 percent of the listed requirements and if your knowledge of the position tells you that you can do the job with the credentials you have.

Remember, most pro football coaches will say they want their quarterback to be six feet four inches and weigh 230 pounds, but they become a bit flexible when a Doug Flutie walks in the door.

Your Local College

Your local college or university is an outstanding traditional source of jobs that not many people take advantage of. Most colleges have a well-established and well-equipped placement office, which is primarily used by that college's senior class. But most college placement offices do not require you to be a student or graduate of that college to take advantage of their services. You would do well to regularly visit this office, become familiar with its resources, and build a relationship with its staff.

Nonprofit Organizations

Let me add another fine source for you. There are many nonprofit organizations—especially churches—that offer outstanding job-search programs. These include seminars, workshops, and great networking meetings, as well as a positive environment for you to work with other people in your same situation. Look in your local newspaper for listings of these programs; they are often listed in the weekend edition under a heading such as "Community Activities."

The Nontraditional Job Market

Eighty percent of all available jobs are never advertised. Let that soak in a moment.

Now think about this: 85 percent of the people looking for jobs only look for them in the traditional advertised job market.

Do the math: 85 percent of the job seekers are chasing 20 percent of the jobs. That is why you have had such a tough time. It is because there is enormous competition for a relatively few number of jobs being advertised.

What you want to do is take yourself out of the 85:20 dogfight and operate in the 15:80 world. You want to be one of the 15 percent looking at 80 percent of the jobs. There are three good methods for doing this: the *Network Referral System*, *door knocking*, and *pulling an inside job.*

The Network Referral System

For every job in the newspaper and other traditional sources, there are four available elsewhere. And the source for these jobs involves much less competition. Instead of three hundred competitors, you are looking at a handful or, quite often, no competitors. What is this source? The coffeepot.

Most jobs are filled at the coffeepot. Here's a typical example: Harry Jenkins is the production manager for a medium-sized computer company. He's had his share of problems today.

Harry decides to take a break and heads to the coffeepot. As he pours a cup, Tom Watkins, the plant's payroll chief, walks up. "Hey, Harry, how's it going?" Tom says with cheer.

Harry is not so gleeful. "I've had better days. Problems at home, machines crashing, budgets due, and my assistant's sick. And to top it off, my software supervisor just quit. Say, do you know anyone who can take that job?"

> Who seeks, and will not take when once 'tis offr'd, shall never find it more.
>
> —William Shakespeare

Tom pauses as he stirs the coffee and replies, "You know, I just talked to someone a couple of weeks ago that might be a good fit. His name is Mike Davison. You ought to talk to him."

"Great," Harry replies. "Give me his number. I'll call him." Tom digs out the number and gives it to Harry. Harry makes the call, sets up an interview, and hires Mike a week later. He never gets around to running a newspaper ad.

Far-fetched? Dumb luck? No. This is how most jobs are filled these days. You can call it the good-old-boy network or lucky happenstance, but it is not. This referral and subsequent job offer resulted from the candidate's wise planning and preparation. He had built a network, and that network paid off.

> A wise man will make more opportunities than he finds.
>
> —Francis Bacon

Right now you are thinking, *I don't know anybody like Tom Watkins. My network is quite small, and it certainly doesn't include people with that kind of influence.* At the moment this may be true. The key in this example and thousands just like it is that the successful job candidate *built* his network. Until two weeks earlier, Mike Davison had never even met Tom Watkins. Yet here is Tom, referring a job offer for him.

This job campaign system has many names: networking, informational interviewing, referral interviewing, and the "secret job market." Large career-consulting companies base their methods (and their $10,000 fees!) on this very system.

Let's take a brief look at the system that will probably lead to your next job. We will continue using Mike Davison's job search as our example.

Mike's last job was as a production supervisor for a company he had worked for his entire career. His job was eliminated when the company was bought out by a competitor.

Mike had been quite focused on his job. While this helped him build an excellent record of promotion, he failed to build any contacts outside of his own company. In fact, the only interest he really pursued outside of work was a fascination with computers; it became a hobby that led to some strong expertise.

Since Mike had not been paying attention to the job market in his industry, he needed some advice. There were things he didn't know about production, new directions it was taking, and who all the key players and companies were. The Network Referral System (NRS) was ideal for his situation.

> No great man ever complains of want of opportunity.
>
> —Ralph Waldo Emerson

First, make a list. Mike made a list of everyone he knew who would have some acquaintance with production management. At first the list was quite short, but it grew as he realized that there were many people who had *some* knowledge or relationship to people in the industry. For instance, one contact he listed was not working for a production company but did business with several that were. The list grew even further when he included people he knew outside of work, such as a friend he had met while shopping for computer software.

Then, make appointments. He called the folks on the list and made appointments to discuss his many questions. For the most part, it was easy to get appointments. Everyone was eager to advise him. Occasionally, there was some resistance. Some contacts thought he was trying to apply for a job or expected them to know of specific jobs. Mike assured them that he was not looking for a job offer yet. In fact, he had a great deal to learn before he could apply with specific companies. Since he was sincerely seeking only advice, the vast majority of those he called eagerly set aside time to see him.

Meet with your network. He prepared a list of questions. At the meetings, he would briefly tell the person about himself and his goals. He asked the questions he had prepared, listened carefully to the advice, and engaged in interesting business conversations.

Mike was careful never to exceed the time allotted, usually thirty minutes. He ended the discussions with "Thank you. You have been a big help. I'd like to learn more about the industry. Who else do you think I should be talking to?" Nearly everyone gave him the names of two or three people. Mike added them to his list and easily made appointments to see them.

It was at one of these appointments (with the casual friend he met at the computer store) that he was referred to Tom Watkins. Tom was not involved in production, but since he was involved with payroll accounting, he might be able to give some insight into current pay scales and the status of credentials the industry might now require. Their joint interest in computers led to an easy, friendly conversation. While it was enjoyable, Mike didn't think it would lead much further because Tom really didn't know much about production. In fact, he hadn't even given any referrals.

> You are not inconveniencing someone when you ask for her advice. You are paying her a high compliment.

Mike thanked him, promised to keep him advised of his career development, and moved on to discussions with the other people he had met in his rapidly expanding network. As he was about to leave to go to another networking meeting, the phone rang. It was Harry Jenkins. "I just talked with a coworker, Tom Watkins. He suggested you and I should meet."

"But I Just Don't Know Anybody!"

Right now you may be thinking, *I can't call some of these people. That fellow from college, sure we were close friends back then, but we never kept in touch. I'd be embarrassed to call him up and ask him to give me some job advice!*

I'll answer you this way: if that fellow were to call you tonight and ask for an hour of your time for some career advice, what would you say? Of course you'd help him. So why would you think he'd have any different reaction? The same logic applies to neighbors and members of your house of worship. If you are like me, I would be insulted if my advice would be helpful to a neighbor but she failed to contact me.

You are not inconveniencing someone when you ask for her advice. You are paying her a high compliment.

Going on a Network Referral Meeting

You got the meeting and are walking through the door. Now what? First, let's remember what must *not* take place:

- This is not a job interview.
- You should have no expectation that the person you are meeting with even knows of a job opening.
- There is no grade; you will not pass or fail this meeting. Relax; it's a business discussion. Really.

What *do* you want to accomplish? Your agenda is limited and specific:

- You want to meet people in your potential industry and build a business relationship with them.
- You want some questions answered.
- You want some advice.
- You would like some referrals.

That is your complete agenda for today. As long as you sincerely approach it that way, you will be relaxed and thoroughly enjoy the meeting. So will the person you are meeting with.

You may have noticed that, unlike all the other sections of this book, I have gone into great detail about this system. There is a reason. The program works. Your universe will expand dramatically, and your name will be available at dozens of coffeepot meetings. So if this program is so effective, why doesn't everyone use it? Because it requires discipline, hard work, and persistence. Most people do not possess all these traits.

Be assured that if you do provide the discipline this system requires, you will end up with the job you want and in a far shorter time than it would take you responding to newspaper ads.

Door Knocking

Door knocking reflects a simple principle. Instead of working through the company and its bureaucracy, you make direct contact with the person who will be your potential boss. In order to understand why this concept works, you must first understand the flow of paper through a company.

When a letter is sent to a company, it is first opened by the mailroom or the receptionist. If a résumé falls out of the envelope, the inquiry is forwarded to the human resources department, no matter who the letter was addressed to. Your inquiry is added to that tall stack we previously discussed. HR does an initial screening—usually by an intern or an entry-level person. This screening lasts approximately ten to thirty seconds. Do you think this intern is looking for reasons to include you in the search? Of course not. She is looking for reasons to *exclude* you and to whittle the stack down to a more manageable size. What gets you excluded? Just about anything will do, really. Your age, your education may not be an exact match (English degree instead of journalism), perceived income needs, *even where you live.*

Let me give you an example of that last one. I know of a young lady who lived in South Carolina but wanted to relocate to Atlanta. (Doesn't everyone?) She applied to several jobs she had seen in the Atlanta newspaper—and these were jobs she was perfectly matched for—but had not received a single response.

My theory? Newspaper ads can, as mentioned, draw as many as a thousand responses. Screening them is a huge, tedious chore usually delegated to the lowest level in HR, often an unpaid intern. The intern is looking for ways to screen people out and uses his ten to thirty seconds to find folks to knock out. Knowing that some people pull out a shotgun and blast their résumés to every ad they can find (on the off chance something might happen), he assumes that my friend from South Carolina is doing just that. Job is in Atlanta, résumé from South Carolina . . . knockout! Move on to the next envelope.

When you send a company a résumé, it will be routed to the HR department. You'll get your ten seconds of consideration, just like the other 999 received that week. But if you use a marketing letter and the direct contact system, you will bypass the intern and be considered by the person who could be your next boss.

What is this magical document called a "marketing letter"? A marketing letter is a combination of a résumé and a cover letter. It is addressed to the decision maker, is well written, and contains accomplishments that fit the position. A marketing letter "targets" a specific employer and job, rather than being a general "broadcast" letter sent in a mass mailing. It can be used even if there is no job available, when the candidate wants an informational interview with a decision maker.

A marketing letter is similar in concept to a direct advertising flyer. It must rivet attention by selling "benefits" to the buyer and can be designed with bullet points to draw the eye down to key points.

The sole goal of a marketing letter is to get an interview. If an employer who wants a more detailed résumé contacts you, you have an opportunity to have phone contact with the individual.

In many cases, a résumé becomes unnecessary once you have your foot in the door.

Here is an example of a marketing letter:

Good morning, Mr. Scott!

While your innovative products have revolutionized the industry, the tight economy has shriveled up the capital expenditure budgets of many of your customers. Their inability to invest at this time has stifled your sales growth at the very time you are best able to address their needs.

I have an extensive history of sales in the capital equipment industry, as well as strong knowledge of financing. In fact, over the past ten years, I have addressed many issues similar to those your company faces right now. Here are some major hurdles I have overcome recently:

- Led a project team, which placed $200 million in communications equipment in a Third World nation, including system design, installation, training, and funding.
- Arranged municipal bond sales for the state of New York that allowed completion of contracts covering the state's payroll system.
- Opened accounts with three major hardware manufacturers, none of which had ever been successfully sold to in our company's history.
- Set annual, quarterly, and monthly sales records for the past three years.

I am looking for an opportunity to solve some more sales problems, engineer a dramatic sales program, and find ways to get your equipment into your customers' factories. I can impact your bottom line and would be excited to tell you how I would do it.

I will call you in a few days to set up a meeting where we can discuss ways I can address your needs.

Sincerely,

To whom do you write? The real trick to this system is not writing the letter. The challenge is finding the right person to write to. With the proliferation of Web directories, company Web pages, and published directories, it should be easy to learn exactly whom to send your letter to. Actually, your easiest and best source of this information is to just call the company directly. Find out who your boss or boss's boss would be, and send the letter directly to that person.

What makes it work? So, you write a Pulitzer-level letter and send it to the right people, yet your phone has not rung. Not once. Lousy system? No, deficient follow-through. No one will read your letter and then call you. Ain't gonna happen. The only way for this to work is for you to follow up with every person you write. You must do this, no exception.

Understand that the immediate odds are still quite long. What are the chances you will contact someone at the exact moment she needs to hire you? Not very good at all.

But what are the odds that if you contact a hundred targeted employers, you will talk to at least one person at the exact moment he needs to hire you? A whole lot better.

And what are the odds that if you contact a hundred targeted employers, you will talk with someone who may need you in six to eight weeks? Pretty darn good.

Do not waste your time sending a letter unless you are committed to follow up. You must follow up with everyone you write. Make their acquaintance and add them to your network.

Stay in touch every month or so, and the odds swing dramatically to your favor.

Pulling an Inside Job

What if you want to switch careers, but have little or no experience in your desired field? A friend recounts this experience:

> I was an employment interviewer. I liked the company and enjoyed my job, but I really wanted to have a career in marketing. But, I had no marketing experience and my degree was not even in business.
>
> Our company had a policy of posting job openings before opening them to the general public. One day, a notice came through for a new entry-level position in marketing. Had I applied for this same job as an external candidate, my résumé would have never even made it past the screener. But since I was an existing employee, people knew me, my temperament, and my work habits. They were willing to give me the opportunity, and now I am on the career track I was hoping for.

I worked my way up from the mailroom is not just a cliché; it is the accurate description for many corporate executives. Insiders have a decided edge in getting open positions. If you have discovered a company you want to be a part of, secure a job—just about any job—with that company. Make contacts, demonstrate your capabilities, and keep your eyes open for the opportunities that spring up.

Also, getting your foot in the door extends beyond the example just given. You don't have to be a regular employee to gain an inside advantage. You can make your presence known via college internships. A fabulous way to walk through the back door is through temping. Again, you don't have to temp in the same job or even department that you are interested in. Just get an assignment that lasts long enough for you to meet the right people and to learn how the inside posting is handled.

Yet another way to get inside from the outside is to be a vendor. I have received several employment offers from companies for which I have consulted or delivered retention seminars. Sell a company its office products and you will eventually become one of the family. Chat with the people you serve, learn their problems, and you will find the occasion to be recruited as if you were already one of them.

Uncle Daniel survived that Great Flood of 1990. Fortunately, it enhanced his prayer life and his faith in the Almighty. He learned to ask for what he needed and trust that it would be delivered. He figured he would save everyone a lot of time and prayed fervently for God to let him win the lottery the following weekend. In fact, he prayed nearly nonstop for the entire week. His faith was once again crushed Saturday evening when he did not win. "Why, Lord? Why did You once again not answer my prayers?" he cried toward the heavens. A powerful voice answered: "For crying out loud, Dan. Meet Me halfway on this. At least buy a lottery ticket."

We've learned three methods for getting that perfect job. They are:

- Letting the problem of "it's all in who you know" actually work *for* you by using *The Network Referral System*
- Approaching companies directly by *Door Knocking*
- Moving from supplier or temp to gainful employment by *Pulling an Inside Job*

These methods will succeed but require a tremendous amount of work from you. And that is why these systems put the odds in your favor—85 percent of the job seekers will not make the effort needed. Your hard work will pay off.

12

MARKET YOURSELF

TOM, LOOK AT THIS ONE," SUSAN SAID AS THEY WERE reviewing résumés for an important new position. "I think this might be our man."

Tom looked over the résumé carefully. At first he was perplexed. "How can you say that? This guy has no experience in the field, has an erratic job history, and never even finished high school." But then he paused, a smile came over his face, and he enthusiastically agreed with Susan. "Yes, *yes*!" Tom replied. "He *is* perfect!" It took him some time, but Tom eventually saw what Susan had noticed: While all of the other candidates had been flaunting their credentials on off-white paper, using one-inch margins and Times New Roman typeface, this man used bright white 24# paper, 1.25-inch margins, and Arial typeface with 12-point Century Gothic captions!

Tom and Susan immediately called the candidate, Bob, who was sitting confidently by the phone, expecting the sizable job offer that they made him. "*You da man!*" they screamed again and again.

Bob was so glad he bought that book on how to write a job-winning résumé.

Your Résumé

That story never happened. But if you read one of the many résumé books, you will think this a typical day at the office. We'll spend a bit of time on this in a minute, but for now, please understand that these subtle differences in presenting yourself will not have any impact on your getting the job you want.

There is nothing that is more misunderstood in the job-hunting process than the use of a résumé. Its use and format are routinely mangled, even by professionals.

Every bookstore has dozens of titles advertising "job-winning résumés" or their status as "the complete résumé book." If you have the right résumé, the implication is, all you have to do is mail it in, the HR manager will read it, and someone will call you and tell you when to report to work. Less ambitious pitchmen will merely tell you that a résumé only serves as a means of getting you an interview, but you have to win the job by responding brilliantly to the interviewer's questions.

In these areas, conventional wisdom is completely wrong.

Here is the real story on résumés. First, no one has ever gotten hired based solely on his or her résumé. And no qualified person was ever denied a job solely because of the résumé. The résumé is important and can be used to give you a powerful advantage. But it is not the whole ball game.

While some people will tell you that the purpose of a résumé is to get an interview, I find this a bit incomplete. Yes, the *initial* purpose is to get you through the screening process, and this is indeed a critical use of it. A résumé is also the document used throughout the hiring process. Every person involved in interviewing you will be given a copy of your résumé. (This is a good reason to make sure your résumé photocopies well, by the way.) So not only does your résumé get you past the screener, it is also the first impression of you for everyone involved in your hiring process.

Let me also get ahead of myself a bit and tell you about another benefit of a well-written résumé. Most interviewers don't know how to interview. This is not their regular job, and they just haven't given much thought to the process. For example, you may interview with a potential supervisor. He may have been busy, had no time to prepare questions, and decided to wing it. (Frankly, about half your interviews will be like this.) Then you walk in, shake hands, and immediately hand him a copy of your résumé. He will use it as an outline for interviewing you. Think about this—you just took complete control of the process. Instead of saying, "Tell me about yourself," he will look at your résumé and say something like, "It says here that you headed up the initial sales campaign for Crispy Chips. Tell me about that." And then you proceed to tell him about all the great things you have accomplished. This gives you an incredible home-field advantage.

> Credentials are not the same as accomplishments.
>
> —Robert Half

The résumé will not get you a job all by itself, but it is obviously a critical and powerful tool. So, how do you write a magnificent résumé? I'm not going to tell you. The bookstores are overflowing with books discussing the construction and mechanics of résumé writing. I can add nothing to the general process.

However, I do have a lot to say about the editing process and resolving some of the many questions about writing a good résumé. Let me use this space to comment on these issues, provide some guidance in the process, and offer meaningful editing recommendations.

Measurable Accomplishments

The highlight of your résumé, its very purpose, should be to highlight what you have accomplished. Education, job titles, and lists of sparkling traits speak to your potential, but accomplishments demonstrate what you have done and can do.

I recommend a format that lists by bullet point the notable accomplishments in your career. These should indeed be noteworthy achievements, not just rewording of job duties. Contrast these examples for a development manager:

- Responsible for new construction and remodeling projects
- Opened fourteen new stores in three years, a company record

While the first example addresses a job description, the second actually speaks to your accomplishment and is far more powerful.

"But I Haven't Really Done Anything Special"

While volunteering at a career ministry, I worked with a middle-aged man looking for a job as an in-city truck driver. I mentioned to him that he should emphasize his accomplishments. "I'm just a truck driver," he said. "I haven't accomplished anything." No amount of prodding could budge him from this meager self-evaluation. Later, over a cup of coffee, he casually mentioned, "You know, I've driven over a million miles and never had an accident or even a traffic ticket." I practically leaped out of my skin as I explained to him that this was a remarkable accomplishment—as well as a marketable one. "Do you realize how many trucking company executives will have written a huge check to their insurance company just before picking up your résumé?"

Another time I was working with a young lady who wanted to apply for a job as an office manager in a dentist's office. After massive tooth pulling, I was eventually able to extract this bullet point:

- Has not been late or absent for a single day of work in six years, despite raising three young children

Sometimes we take for granted the accomplishments that will most impress our employers. Spend some time making your list of accomplishments, and evaluate them based on how the *employer* will perceive them.

Focus on the Specific Job

Your résumé should speak directly to the hiring manager reading it. You want to highlight your skills and achievements in ways that are relevant to the position you're applying for. Customize your résumé so that it targets the specific job you are seeking.

Since each résumé should be customized for the specific job you are applying for, your *accomplishments* should also be customized. For example, if your previous position was as a sales manager for a software company, you may be led to apply for three different types of jobs: sales, management, and IT. Compose five or six bullet points for each of these subdisciplines. Customize your résumé by including all five of the bullet points for the specific subcategory you are applying for and two or three of the others.

The Format

There are two basic résumé formats. The traditional format is *chronological.* This lists jobs in reverse order, most recent job first. HR people like this format, because it clearly shows career progression as well as how long you stayed at each job. For most people, this is the easiest and clearest way to present their credentials. However, the chronological résumé works against some people. Gaps in employment are easy to spot, and short tenure jumps off the page, labeling you as a job-hopper. And since it focuses on job titles, a chronological résumé works against you when you are trying to change careers.

To address these issues, some people choose a *functional* format, which summarizes your career by listing skills and accomplishments. Some functional résumés don't even include company names, job titles, or dates. While this format is an excellent way to highlight your skills for career changes and to cover up job-hopping, you should never use a purely functional résumé format. Most employers will think you are trying to hide something. A functional résumé format might seem to be the answer to your credential problems, but it will almost always get you eliminated from any further consideration.

> Yes, but if "less is more" think how much more "more" would be.
>
> —Dr. Frasier Crane

So, what to do? Again, most people should use the traditional chronological résumé. Interviewers like it, and if you have not job-hopped, it will not raise any eyebrows. But if you do need to change careers or deal with issues, there is a solution: the *combined* format.

A combined résumé (sometimes called the *semifunctional*) combines both chronological and functional formats. This is usually a two-page résumé. On the first page, you list areas of expertise and ten to fifteen significant accomplishments in your career. These accomplishments, as well as the areas of expertise, are selected to support your credentials for the new job you want.

On the second page, you list your previous positions, along with company name, job title, and dates of employment. These are listed without any fanfare, such as job descriptions or accomplishments (which were highlighted on the first page).

While all the "incriminating" information is still included on your résumé (making the HR department happy), it is not highlighted such that it becomes the focus of your document. The focus—or should I say the *advertisement*?—is clearly on your skills and accomplishments.

Less Is More

Back in 1933, my great-aunt Halle ran a telegraph office in Kentucky. One afternoon, a collie walked in, took out a blank form, and wrote, *Woof. Woof woof woof. Woof woof. Woof. Woof. Woof.* My aunt examined the paper and politely told the dog: "There are only nine words here. You could send another *Woof* for the same price."

"But," the dog replied, "that would make no sense at all."

Make your résumé as simple and easy to read as possible. Avoid gimmicks, multiple fonts, and lots of adjectives. Limit your information. You are writing a summary and a brief advertisement, not an autobiography. Give them just enough *woofs*, and provide the details at the interview.

You are writing a summary and a brief advertisement, not an autobiography. Give them just enough *woofs*, and provide the details at the interview.

Telephone Number

List only telephone numbers at which you can talk freely. Yes, this sounds obvious, but you would be shocked at the number of times I have dialed a number on a résumé, only to be told that I should not have called the person at the office.

Don't get cute with your answering machine message. What

sounds funny or sexy when a friend calls sounds absolutely unprofessional when a potential employer listens to it. I have called people and gotten messages beginning with "Hey, baby," the theme from *Star Wars*, and rude noises. Remember, every telephone line becomes a business phone when listed on a résumé. Make sure it upholds the image.

E-Mail Address

List your e-mail address prominently on your résumé. Many employers like to use e-mail as a first contact or to send you information. It is difficult to give an e-mail address verbally, so make it easy to find this information. Put it right there with your street address and telephone numbers.

Make certain that the e-mail address you give is a personal address. Never, ever use your company e-mail for a job search. Obvious? Ten percent of the résumés I get list a company e-mail.

Also, keep your screen name professional. What image is projected by e-mail addresses such as *morebeer*, *sexydude*, and *hounddawg*? Certainly not that of someone I would want to hire to run my business. And keep it simple. *Brsmith211966* is just too complicated.

You can obtain an e-mail account easily and at no cost. Consider having an e-mail account to be used for your job search only.

Job Objective

A typical résumé will begin with a job objective that goes something like this: *I am looking for a company that will . . .* This is a mistake. The fact is, no company cares what you want *from* it; the managers are looking for what you can do *for* them. From that perspective, "job objective" shouldn't even be on the résumé. Save this for the cover letter.

If you do choose to put a job objective on your résumé, it had better exactly match the job you are seeking. If it varies in the slightest, you will have handed the HR clerks the excuse they are seeking to toss you into the circular file. Best advice: leave off the job objective. Second-best advice: rewrite the job objective on every résumé you send out, ensuring that it matches the job you are applying for. But realize that this may eliminate the possibility that you may be considered for other positions in the organization.

How Far Back?

I recently received a résumé from a fellow who had been a company president for the last ten years and a senior executive for five years before that. But he didn't stop there. His résumé took him back almost thirty years, listing his first job as a dishwasher in a restaurant.

> I have never seen a bad résumé.
>
> —John Y. Brown

A résumé is not a biography. It should not list everything about you and your life. It should list only those things that a potential employer would find of interest. Listing too many jobs and going back too far simply dilute your accomplishments.

A good rule of thumb is to go back fifteen years or three companies, whichever gives the best picture of you and your career progression. If you have previous jobs or accomplishments you would like to highlight, create an entry under "Selected Accomplishments" or "Personal." (This is a good place to mention that you are a veteran or to highlight some earth-shattering accomplishment you had very early in your career.) The farther back you go, the less space you have to tout your more recent accomplishments.

Job Duties

Consider this entry for Babe Ruth:

New York Yankees
Right Fielder
- Caught fly balls, threw them back into the infield.
- Hit baseballs, preferably over the fence.
- Ran bases (counterclockwise).

My point: Most job titles do not need a lot of clarification, especially when the job titles are fairly consistent within the industry. If the duties are obvious, don't use valuable space to describe them. Instead, use the space to highlight accomplishments. Consider this revision:

New York Yankees
- Elected to Hall of Fame on first ballot.
- Set numerous records that stood for decades, including home runs in a career and in a season.
- Had candy bar named after me.
- Was subject of motion picture in which I saved a cute little puppy.

Job duties rarely need to be explained. Instead, use the space to emphasize how you used those duties to get things done.

Personal

Most gurus will tell you to leave off personal information, such as hobbies, family status, or club memberships. Here is their logic: you are giving out information that someone might use to discriminate against you or to screen you out. While I generally agree with that line of logic, I am going to reverse myself a bit and recommend that you *sometimes* include carefully selected personal information. Why? A couple of reasons.

First, there are some prejudices that might work in your favor, but the employer can't ask you about them. For instance, most employers look favorably upon a stable family life. Technically, the employer cannot ask about your family, but there is no law preventing you from volunteering the information. *Married twelve years with three daughters* sends a message to the employer that he could not ask you about directly. Likewise, employers are not allowed to ask you if you have any children, but don't you think that raising three small children would be looked upon with favor if you were applying to run a day care?

Another reason I recommend including certain personal information is that it can serve as an icebreaker at the interview. Remember, most interviewers are not adept at interviewing, so the initial few moments can be awkward. Perhaps the interviewer will see "Hobbies include golf . . ." on your résumé and will use that to break the ice.

Still another reason for personal information is that you may have an opportunity to bond with the interviewer. Here is a shocking but true fact: most interviewers make up their minds about you in the first two minutes. Perhaps the interviewer was born in France, and your résumé includes the personal fact that you once traveled extensively through Europe. This is a bonding opportunity.

So include hobbies, a solid marriage, spouse's occupation, and civic memberships in the personal section when you see them as opportunities for generating positive conversations.

Avoid controversial entries. I once served as executive secretary for a gun-control advocacy group. As proud as I am of this service, I avoided listing it on my résumé; there was too great a chance that a potential employer would silently veto me just because he held a differing view of the Second Amendment. (It is my contention that the Second Amendment contains a typo. I believe our founding fathers actually wanted to allow citizens to arm bears.) Civic involvement is a credit to your leadership skills, and you can allude to it in your résumé. Just take care in identifying controversial causes.

> A bad reference is as hard to find as a good employee.
>
> —Robert Half

Education

Don't lie. Does this seem obvious? Perhaps, but it is one of the most fudged-about items on a résumé. It is also the easiest to verify. It costs the employer nothing to verify your educational claims, and colleges will give out this information without requesting any permission slip from you. The employer doesn't even need a social security number! I have seen many job offers withdrawn and several people fired because they listed nonexistent degrees. Further, suppose you do get away with it. It will be hanging over your head forever; you'll be looking over your shoulder constantly, worried that the new HR guy will decide to verify credentials.

Omit Boilerplate

There are things placed on résumés just because people have seen them on other résumés and think they are supposed to be there. "Excellent health" and "References available upon request" are tired entries that only weaken the impact of your résumé. These are clichés, and you should avoid using clichés like the plague.

Fighting Age Discrimination

Those of you who have read my previous books on recruiting and retention know how furious this subject makes me. I won't retread that ground here. (But it's worth the twenty-five bucks to buy those books just to hear me rant.) But let me give you some ways to deal with this issue on your résumé.

Fifty-year-olds will not be able to fool any employer who is outwardly trying to discriminate. Even if you hide your age completely on the résumé, you will eventually have to meet the guy, and he'll eliminate you then if that is his inclination. So we are not trying to combat the blatant bigot; we're just trying to de-emphasize age for the latent bigot. Here are some ways:

- Don't go back more than fifteen years on your job history.
- Try to limit the number of jobs listed. For instance, only have a single entry per company rather than treating each promotion or job-title change as a separate entry.
- Don't list dates for your degrees or other credentials.
- Avoid using terms such as *mature*, but do use words like *energetic* and *motivated*.

Of course, anyone who is outwardly trying to discriminate will always find indications on your résumé, no matter how well crafted it is. And eventually, the employer will meet you face-to-face. But that is our goal, because it is much easier to deal with perceived age-related issues in person than on paper.

And Here's Some More Good Stuff...

Let's conclude our résumé discussion with some important remarks about them. Here are six tips for assuring your résumé is as powerful as it can be:

1. *Eliminate all errors*. Résumé screeners will zero in on an error or a typo and blow it completely out of proportion. There is no telling how many people applying for a contractor's job were

eliminated because they wrote *accept* instead of *except*. Proofread, and then give it to two perfectionists to scour it some more.

2. *Highlight specific accomplishments*. Don't be vague (e.g., *Headed remodeling campaign*). Instead, spell out specific, impressive actions, highlighted with solid numbers: *Oversaw all remodeling activities in New York, supervising 5 contractors and a $22 million budget.* The more specific you are with your accomplishments, the more powerful impression you will make.

3. *Show a pattern of career growth*. Do not appear to have a stagnant or erratic career. These mistakes are often made by listing each slight change in responsibility as a new job. Instead, list your jobs in a manner that clearly shows you moving up in responsibility.

4. *Emphasize your compatibility with the job and company*. Even a perfectly written résumé may not express your compatibility with the position. Edit your résumé for each job you seek, emphasizing the skills that will make you fit into this specific job and company culture.

5. *Emphasize your adaptability*. Use the "Personal" section to slip in situations that make you more marketable and don't really fit into other categories. One such powerful entry is, "Available for heavy travel and relocation."

6. *Keep it clear and organized*. This printed piece gives people their first impression of you. If the résumé appears cluttered and unorganized, you will be perceived the same way. Most HR creatures like to see bullet points, lots of white space, and clear explanations of activities, job duties, and accomplishments.

The Cover Letter

The cover letter is another critical document that is almost always misused in the search for a job. I chuckle when I see stacks of books with titles such as *Job-Winning Cover Letters.* (These are on the shelf next to the equally silly books called *Job-Winning Résumés.*) Most cover letters are an exercise in creative writing that tries to create an image that the writer is a glowing visionary. The cover letter gets hung up in the verbiage and fails to serve any logical purpose. Worse, most cover letters take hours to write and are never even read.

> Never hire anybody whose résumé rhymes.
>
> —Robert Wieder

Let's first discuss what a cover letter is *not*. It is not a chance to demonstrate your creative-writing abilities. It is not a place for you to dazzle the reader with your brilliant observations about the direction of the industry and how you can lead the company into the next century. (As I write this, we are well into the twenty-first century, yet I *still* receive cover letters talking about leadership into the *next* century. Are these people truly thinking ninety-four years ahead?) And it is most definitely not a standardized form letter listing a bunch of generalities.

So, what *is* the purpose of a cover letter? Simply, it clearly connects your résumé and credentials to the required profile for this particular job. That's all it does, but this serves a critical role in the hiring process.

You wrote your résumé to be used for several possible positions, and it probably doesn't emphasize all your skills. For instance, if you have been a sales manager for a computer company, you may now be applying for separate jobs in management, sales, and computers. Your résumé touches on each of these disciplines, but a good cover letter will focus on the applicable skill set. It will highlight your sales ability for sales jobs, leadership accomplishments for management jobs, and computer expertise for IT positions. To list all your accomplishments in all three areas on your résumé would make you appear unfocused. Doing so on your cover letter makes you look targeted.

An excellent way to do this is by actually making a T chart on your letter. One side is labeled *Your Desired Qualifications* and the other side *My Experience*. In this way, you will use the company's own words to sell your candidacy. More important, you will sail through the résumé screeners, saving them the effort of digging through your résumé for the proper credentials (which they won't do anyway).

Having just one résumé is acceptable. A "standard cover letter" is actually an oxymoron. Each job requires its own custom introduction. Use the cover letter to tie your résumé to each specific job you apply for.

Using E-mail

Speed and convenience make e-mail the preferred mode for much of today's employment correspondence. For the most part, all the rules for corresponding by mail apply to using e-mail. But there are some differences that we should discuss.

Use a standard word-processing program. If you attach your cover letter or résumé, always use Microsoft Word. Nothing halts a job search like a résumé the recruiter can't read. And please, never be tempted to substitute a PowerPoint presentation for your résumé. You might as well show up in a tutu and sing a jingle in their office.

Please, never be tempted to substitute a PowerPoint presentation for your résumé. You might as well show up in a tutu and sing a jingle in their office.

Use a business font. Most e-mail programs use Courier as the default font. (This is the one that looks like old-fashioned typewriter print.) It makes a weak impression, however. Change the font to a more businesslike one, such as Arial or Times New Roman.

Send it from home. Just as you wouldn't print a cover letter on your company's letterhead, you shouldn't use your employer's e-mail in job correspondence. Yet about 10 percent of the messages I receive are generated on company e-mail programs. This leaves a lousy first impression and may even cause your elimination by some companies. Set up a separate e-mail account for just your job search.

Make good use of the subject line. Recruiters receive tons of e-mails each day from applicants just like you. Virtually all of them have only the word *Résumé* in the subject line. You should make yours stand out. Include your name, the position you're applying for, and any job code. Make it easy for the prospective employer to pick you out of the masses.

Use keywords. Many companies scan résumés before recruiters read them. Applicant tracking systems scan your correspondence for keywords matching the job specification. Tailor your cover letter and résumé to that job spec.

Although no one has ever purchased a new car solely from a spiffy television commercial, there is a reason auto companies spend tens of millions of dollars on that advertising. The ad makes the first impression, frames an image, and gives you reasons to walk through the door of the dealership.

Your marketing documents, particularly the résumé, serve this same purpose. No one will hire you straight from the paperwork, but you will firmly set your first impression. Most further interactions with this company will branch from that piece of paper. Make it your best effort.

The Interview

Cousin Ralph took his uncle Sherlock on a camping trip. Sherlock was an English professor at the local community college, and Ralph figured he could use some of the exposure to the real world that you get while visiting the foothills of the Smokies.

They set up their tent; enjoyed a fine stew; shared an old, classic bottle of root beer; and went right to bed. Several hours later, Ralph woke up and nudged his learned uncle. "Sherlock, look up and tell me what you see."

"I see millions and millions of stars," Sherlock answered.

"And what does that tell you?"

The professor pondered the profound possibilities for a minute and then replied, "Well, astronomically, it tells me that there are millions of galaxies and potentially billions of planets. Astrologically, I observe that Saturn is in Leo. Meteorologically, I suspect that we will have a beautiful day tomorrow. Horologically, I deduce that the time is approximately a quarter past three. Theologically, I can see that God is all-powerful, and that we are a small and insignificant part of the universe. What does it tell you, Ralph?"

Cousin Ralph was silent for a moment and then added his observation: "Well, Uncle Sherlock, all that is probably true. But seeing all those stars tells me just one thing: somebody's done stole our tent."

> The graveyards are full of indispensable men.
>
> —Charles de Gaulle

Some people have a natural tendency to analyze a subject to death. And these "some people" become "most people" when preparing for a job interview. If there are more job-search books on anything besides résumés, it must be instructions for job interviewing. These books offer detailed reviews, a list of the one thousand most popular interview questions *(and job-winning responses!)*, and dissections on how to approach the process. I'm not going to rehash them here or provide you with a complete guide to interviewing. It is just not a good use of your time.

That is not to say that you should neglect to prepare for the interview. Preparation is absolutely critical. But your preparation should involve things that will get you the job, not memorizing staged answers to fancy questions.

Let's review the approach you should take to the interview process and the way you should use your time to prepare for it. Let's begin by simply reviewing your attitude. That's right—it's time to get your attitude adjusted.

Your Attitude and Approach

Get the job offer, and then decide. Remember these words throughout your job-hunting experience.

True, interviewing is a two-way street. Just as the company is attempting to determine whether or not to hire you, you are simultaneously trying to determine whether you want to work there. But it is to your benefit to enter all interviews with an attitude that you absolutely want the job. Why? Because by having that attitude you come off best in the process. Employers can pick up on any reservations you have, any doubts you are feeling, and any disapproval that may be evolving. This analysis can be misinterpreted as hostility and reflect on your personality. Also, people like to feel liked. If the company thinks you are ambivalent, the managers will not be

> You can't turn down a job you are not offered.

excited about bringing you on board. Get the job offer, and then do your analysis.

You can't turn down a job you are not offered. Your best shot at getting the job offer is to project the image that ever since you were a nine-year-old child, you dreamed of being the assistant sales manager for the Midwest region of the nation's third-largest electronic-gizmo manufacturer.

Research the Company

You want to know as much as possible about the company, the job, and the manager before you enter the interview. While basic networking and reading company brochures will tell you a lot, the Internet has opened up an entire new level of performing detective work.

Do a Google search and discover the company Web page as well as references to the company on other sites. If you are fortunate and the company is big enough, you may even find an employee gripe site. It is often useful to know what the company's malcontents have to say. Enter a chat room and get the inside scoop on the company as well as the people with whom you will interview. Also, do a news search on Google, which will display all the newspaper stories written about the company for the past thirty days. Reading them will show that you not only know about the company, but you are current on its public issues.

Dress Appropriately

In a perfect world, potential employers wouldn't care how you dress. Apparently, many people think that we live in a perfect world. They arrive at interviews wearing shorts, T-shirts, and sandals, with their noses pierced and hair a flaming orange. We would like to think that we're being judged on our qualifications, skills, and depth of character. But clothes send a message, and that message is closely scrutinized. To think any other way is to ignore reality.

How do you know what to wear? Ask. The company is used to this question and doesn't consider it strange. Managers know that dress codes vary dramatically and will appreciate your attempt to learn their culture from the get-go.

Arrive at the Right Time

Be there just a few minutes before you are scheduled. It can irk an employer to be told that the candidate for a 10:00 a.m. appointment is waiting in the lobby at 9:35. The employer will feel he is being rushed, and you will disrupt his flow. This will often work against you. You will not score any points by being early, but you could leave the impression that you have nothing else to do with your day. If your appointment is at 2:00, then arrive at 1:50. If this makes you nervous, then go ahead and arrive thirty minutes early. Just wait in the parking lot until interview time.

Do not panic if something unexpected occurs that causes you to be late. Employers will understand freeway gridlock. If you had no control over it or could not have reasonably anticipated the problem, call the employer and ask to reschedule for later the same day. If you arrive just a few minutes late, simply explain the situation to the employer when you arrive. Don't let this get you rattled and ruin the process. Employers will not be bothered by unforeseen problems; they will take note if you appear to panic over relatively minor problems.

Bond with the Interviewer

I do not exaggerate: 95 percent of your success in getting a job boils down to how much the interviewer likes you.

That statement is as true as it is shallow. Your best opportunity for getting the job offer comes from being able to bond with the person who interviews you, particularly if that person is your potential boss. But you must be able to bond with everyone in the process, not just your potential boss. Many a candidate has dropped by the wayside, not because he could not relate to his potential boss, but because things didn't go well with the entry-level HR person who did the initial screening interview.

Your best opportunity for getting the job offer comes from being able to bond with the person who interviews you.

Here are some bonding opportunities:

- Match the interviewer's demeanor. Try to replicate her posture, voice volume, and tone, as well as her pace of breathing. Seriously. You will be amazed at the immediate bond that occurs when two people synchronize their speeds and depth of breathing.
- Look for clues. Look around the office for pictures, knickknacks, and memorabilia that might indicate common interests. Golf clubs or a bowling trophy. A piece of art. College memorabilia. A Seattle Mariners pennant. Family photos. Find something in the office that indicates a common interest or value.
- Listen to comments he makes: "I majored in art history." "My wife teaches fourth grade." "My kid got her tonsils

out." "I went to high school in Denver." The interviewer will make several side comments; listen to them, and look for hooks to your background.

Answer the Questions

As I've stated before, most interviewers don't know how to interview. This isn't as much a statement of disrespect for their abilities as it is a recognition that they don't interview that often. They really haven't gotten the chance to become good at it. Because of this, you will find that many first interviews feature identical questions. Let's not debate the quality of this questioning; let's just use this as an opportunity to prepare for the four types of questions you will be asked.

1. *Résumé questions.* These questions ask about your past experience, business skills, job responsibilities, education, upbringing, and personal interests. In other words, they ask about the things you have listed on your résumé.

Since your résumé consists of facts that tend to be quantifiable and verifiable, these questions require accurate, fact-based answers. Do not exaggerate your achievements or be vague. If properly prepared, your résumé will showcase you nicely, and your answers can reflect confidence in your competence.

> You can't build a reputation on what you are going to do.
>
> —Henry Ford

2. *Skill analysis.* These inquiries will usually be phrased in some sort of superlative, such as: What is your greatest strength? Biggest weakness? Greatest accomplishment? Worst mistake? Interviewers will probably want you to comment on your abilities or assess your past performance. Anticipate these inquiries and prepare for them. Make your responses topic specific

and positive. Try to relate your answer to some aspect of the job being discussed. For instance, "I can use that strength to help me sell your new product line," or "Though it was a whopper of a mistake, I learned from it. And I can use that lesson to help you reorganize your customer-service hotline."

3. *Hypothetical questions.* Interviewers refer to this as behavioral interviewing. It involves questions that ask for examples of how you have handled problems in the past, or maybe how you would address a hypothetical scenario.

> The audience is always right.
>
> —Woody Allen

Pause for a moment and organize your thoughts before answering. The interviewer will learn a great deal about your suitability for the job by your answer. Give an organized response to the scenario, backed up by good examples. Again, try to tie your response to the job being discussed.

4. *Stress questions.* Unless you are being interviewed as a presidential press secretary, these questions are usually unnecessary. Still, amateur interviewers like stress questions because they give them a sense of control.

These questions include the silly: *If you were a tree, what kind of tree would you be?* And the hostile: *What if I told you that I thought your tie looked cheap?* And the profound: *Define the universe and give two examples.* And the most-asked interview question: *Tell me about yourself.*

Stress questions are designed to measure your emotional reflexes while you're under pressure. Since they tend to put you in a defensive posture, the best way to handle them is to recognize the questions for what they are, and give calm, carefully measured answers.

Go ahead and expect the "Tell me about yourself" question.

Most people are stunned and say something like, "Well, there's not much to tell." Prepare a ninety-second response that summarizes your career and states what you are looking for in a new job.

Ask Some Questions

An interview will quickly disintegrate into an interrogation unless you ask some questions of your own. Your questions are critical to a successful interview because they create dialogue. This prevents the interview from being a one-way street. You'll find that the interview becomes more like a conversation between two equals rather than a checklist interrogation.

- Don't ask a question just to ask a question. This point may seem obvious, but many people will ask questions merely to impress the interviewer. Doing this will backfire; the interviewer will see through you, and you'll look shallow.
- Ask questions that reveal the depth of your research and your interest in the job. In other words, don't ask questions that are easily answered on the company Web site or in the job description.
- Don't ask questions about salary until you are offered the job. If you do ask, the interviewer will think you are more interested in the money than in the position. This may be so, but it is hardly the message you want to give.
- Here is one question to always ask—preferably early in the interview: *What makes a successful candidate?* The interviewer will tell you specifically what he is looking for and the responses he expects from you. Follow the lead and shape your answers to address the criteria he outlines for you.

Difficult Interview Situations

Good planning usually makes for a good interview, but sometimes you are thrown a curveball. Let's look at some of the abnormal situations so that you can be prepared for them.

Dealing with Jerks

While we usually work hard to prepare for the ideal interview, we sadly learn that there are few ideal interviewers. As I noted earlier, few people actually train to interview properly. Interviewing is usually just a small part of their jobs, often a bit more than a distraction from their real work. Therefore, you should prepare for the situations that are often referred to as "interviews from hell." Let's review a few of them.

The intimidator. Some people look upon interviewing as an exercise in putting you in your place. What is that place? You are the flea, and the interviewer is the dog's claw. She'll ask questions to make you squirm, and she'll have you sit in a chair that puts your knees up near your ears and the sun in your eyes. She'll keep you waiting far past your scheduled time and let you know right off that you should feel honored to meet her.

What to do? I suggest you leave. No kidding. People should be at their best in an interview, and that works both ways. Do you want to work in a company that allows this person to represent it? Even worse, do you want her as your boss?

You do? OK, in that case, you need to be willing to stroke her ego and let her know that you are willing to subordinate yourself to her. Do not fight her. This person wants to be obeyed, not challenged. If you want the job, show her that you will be compliant and obedient.

The frustrated psychologist. He will ask smarmy questions, like "Is the glass half empty or half full?" (The best answer to this is

"It looks like you've got about twice as much glass as you need.") or "Do you put salt on your food before tasting it?" This person is usually young in his career as an interviewer and is overreaching because he recently read something cute in a management book. This person doesn't know what he is doing but is dangerous because he honestly thinks he does. If he is your potential boss, beware. Do you really want to work for someone like this? If this person is one of the cogs in the process, play along. The "right" answers to the questions will be rather obvious; go with them and get through the process.

The incompetent. These people may have tremendous competence as accountants, supervisors, or scientists. They just have no earthly idea how to conduct an interview. Be kind. While they should have learned how to conduct an interview, they do it so rarely that you should not form a negative opinion about how they perform the rest of their job.

Actually, incompetent interviewers present you with awesome opportunity. Since they don't know what to do, they will have no problem with your taking charge. Do so. Stick your résumé in their hands and they will interview you directly from it: "It says here that you completely turned around the sales in the Northwest Territory. How did you do that?" Think about it. You are being interviewed directly from a document you prepared that highlights all your strengths. As they say in the beer commercials, it doesn't get any better than this.

The poker player. No matter what you say, you just can't seem to get a response. *I was first in my graduating class.* Uh-huh. *I hold a patent in microbiological plasmic recycling.* Hmmm. *I used to be president of Brazil.* That's nice.

Don't try harder. Don't attempt to impress her. That's just not going to happen. You should actually tone it down and speak of your accomplishments in a more matter-of-fact tone. Realize that what you are saying is being noted; it is just not in this person's nature to be expressive. Relax.

The yakker. Don't interrupt. That would be the cardinal sin when dealing with a yakker. Instead, take advantage of the situation. He will ramble on, eventually telling you what he wants to hear. Take note and parrot it back at the appropriate time. If you can get a word in.

Responding to Illegal Questions

I was conducting a telephone interview with a possible candidate for a company I represented and was a bit perplexed about his job history. If he had been younger, his experience would be impressive. But an older candidate should really have had deeper credentials. So I cut to the chase by asking a question that was clearly improper: "How old are you?" He sprang to the offensive and let me know that it was "against the law" to ask him that. In my best Lou Grant imitation, I replied, "You wanna call a cop?"

This is an area where candidates can win the battle but lose the war. Sometimes interviewers ask questions they really shouldn't, but their intent is honest. How does it profit you to point out the mistake and embarrass them? Or even insinuate that you are threatening them? Let honest mistakes and simple questions pass.

> Answer illegal questions with legal answers.

Answer illegal questions with legal answers. If someone asks you, "Do you own a car?" don't make a federal case out of the question; just address his concern. What he really wants to know is whether you have made arrangements to be at work on time every day, so reply, "I will be here every day, on time. I hope you will check my references; they will tell you how dependable I am." He'll get the message plus he'll get the answer he was actually looking for.

During a Meal

Breaking bread is one of the most human social symbols. Being asked to share a meal late in the interview process is a great sign; it shows that you are being invited into the family. In any event, meal interviews require special considerations. Consider these tips:

- Don't get off track. Being at a dinner will make you relax and let your guard down. Since it is a social setting, you may start to think of the event as social rather than business. Always keep it top of mind that you are at an interview. You are meeting your future boss, not an old college buddy.
- Don't smoke, even if your host does. Drink alcohol only if your host does and only if you would normally drink on these occasions. (Don't take up drinking just because you want to "bond" with the interviewer.) And never consume more than two drinks, regardless of what your host does.
- Display impeccable manners. Don't be a snob or a stiff, but do demonstrate that you know how to carry yourself in social situations.
- Treat the waitstaff with respect. 'Nuff said.
- Order food that is easy to eat. No lobster, spaghetti, or French onion soup.
- Breakfast meetings rarely involve the consumption of much food. You will be looked upon with great suspicion if you order a western omelet and double hash browns. Order coffee and a muffin, then take only one nibble from the muffin. You should probably stop by McDonald's on the way there, just so you are not hungry during the interview.

Getting the Last Word

One morning, Cousin Ralph accidentally put a bowl of instant grits in the microwave and briefly went back in time. Fortunately, he traveled to the previous day's job interview and was able to give a brilliant answer to a question he had previously fumbled.

In every interview, there is at least one question that you wish you could take another shot at. Or as you were leaving, you remembered something brilliant you wish you had said. Or you wonder whether or not you were really clear in an important point you wanted to make. The grits-in-the-microwave trick rarely works, so here is an alternate way to completely reverse an earlier fumble: make good use of the thank-you letter.

After your brief thank-you for the person's time, add a remark such as, "I was thinking about our interesting discussion about foreign oil subsidies and recalled . . ." Then pontificate intelligently on the very subject you fumbled during the interview. The routine thank-you letter gives you the chance to write and write your answer until it is exactly what you want to say. And because it is in writing, your "brilliant" observation will stick with the person far longer than the memory of your previously weak verbal response. Use the thank-you letter as the opportunity to turn a weak spot in your interview into a powerful final impression.

As promised, my advice for interviewing has avoided the paralyzing analysis of the Q&A session. Rather than spending hours memorizing clichéd answers to the "1000 top interview questions," I want you to use your time to learn about the job and company, assure a great first impression, and prepare to demonstrate how your qualifications match the job to be filled.

You will be more likely to get the job and, besides, you won't have to think so darn hard.

13

BOUNCE BACK

ALTHOUGH IT NEVER SEEMS SO AT THE TIME, LOSING YOUR job is sometimes the best thing that will ever happen to you. Winston Churchill reflected on this after being voted out of office after leading England to a great victory in World War II. Responding to his wife's declaration that his job loss might be a "blessing in disguise," Churchill replied, "If it is, then it is very effectively disguised."

But his wife was probably right. After all, look at what happened to Ronald Reagan after being released by Hollywood, or Lee Iacocca after Henry Ford dumped him, or Famous Amos when he was forced to start his own business. Consider Golda Meir, who was fired as a librarian in Milwaukee and immigrated to Israel, eventually becoming its prime minister. One more: Walt Disney went out on his own after being fired for "not having any good ideas."

The fact is that losing one's job is often the only way some people can be motivated to discover better, more exciting opportunities. Without the proper kick in the pants, many people would spend their entire existence in the same company, doing the same work, their entire careers.

However, I am aware that most people do not regard job loss with such glee. Let's look at some common scenarios of career disasters and successful strategies for bouncing back from them.

Layoffs and Downsizings

One of the hardest career setbacks to accept is losing your job when it is not your fault. Corporations make liberal use of layoffs these days, softening the horror by using a friendly term such as *downsizing*.

No matter how pleasantly labeled, losing your job in a corporate downsizing is traumatic. Let's look at how you can see it coming and even take action to save yourself.

How to Know if a Layoff Is Coming

Let's look back at some recent economic history. Remember the booming job picture of the 1990s? If you could fog a mirror, you had your choice of jobs. Then came a period when jobs in certain industries disappeared, prompted primarily by the dot-com bust. Millions of highly skilled people scrambled for any work they could find. This was followed by a gradual recovery as workers made their way back into the workforce, often in reshaped career paths.

I don't know what the state of the economy will be when you read these words, but you can be assured that the economy will go through about a dozen economic cycles during your career. It would be wise to learn how to recognize the signs of a company contemplating layoffs.

> Crisis molds and shapes a man's character.
>
> —Richard Nixon

See the writing on the wall. Most people who are laid off never see it coming. That's sad because the warning signs are almost always there and are easy to pick up if you keep your ear to the ground. Pay attention to changes around the office; often the signs are not subtle. These are some signs that your company may be in trouble, placing your job at risk:

- Your company is having declining earnings, losing market share, selling assets, or acquiring debt.
- Companies in your industry are laying off workers.
- The company begins to issue new, highly restrictive financial policies and begins unusual penny-pinching strategies that really don't have a major effect on corporate cash flow. For instance, new travel policies cut per diems by 5 percent, or the company stops furnishing free coffee. When a financial situation seems out of control, executives feel the need to do something—*anything*—and you'll see a flurry of knee-jerk reactions resulting from this panic.
- People are hired from outside the company, and they bring in their own teams.
- Key executives begin leaving the company for no obvious reason.
- A hiring freeze is declared. This is often a failing company's last-ditch effort to reduce staff through attrition. While it does show that a company is resisting layoffs, it's also a sign that the company believes its payroll is too large and its people are the cause of its problem. This is often a first step toward massive layoffs. Hiring freezes make it psychologically easier for the company to begin ridding itself of people. It's hard to jump right in and lay off a large part of the workforce, but a hiring freeze often begins the slippery slope that makes mass layoffs more palatable for the people making these decisions.
- Training programs are cut back. Be alarmed when a company cuts back on the development of its people. This is a warning sign not only of the company's financial issues, but also of a long-term management philosophy that will have a grave impact on your career even if you are not laid off.

Perhaps the best way to find out if a layoff is coming is to ask. Approach your boss or boss's boss, and tell her what is on your mind. You will get a straight answer, or she will have a deer-in-the-headlights look. Management is not good at lying about these things.

Perhaps the best way to find out if a layoff is coming is to ask.

If You See It Coming . . .

There are ways to prevent being a victim of a reduction in force. People are not selected randomly. Usually, a reduction in force simply slices off a percentage of workers at each level and in each department.

Here are some strategies that may save your neck:

- *Improve performance.* The number one criterion in a selection process is performance. Approach your boss and ask if she has observed any deficiencies and ways you can improve your performance. Sometimes, shortcomings in performance can be compensated for by an attitude of wanting to improve. This gesture will be in your boss's mind when she selects the people to be voted off the island.
- *Ask to do more.* Reductions in force are done to decrease the number of workers, but the work remains. People who survive must be able to handle more work and responsibility. Again, do a preemptive strike. Approach your boss and ask for a greater workload. Show him how you can handle more responsibility. He will certainly remember this effort when he evaluates who is critical to the company's post-layoff future.
- *Request a transfer.* Another big criterion for determining who gets laid off is seniority. There is nothing you can

> Success is just as sweet the second time around.
>
> —Dave Thomas

do about this, right? Wrong. Most layoffs are done office by office or by department. If you have low seniority in your current workgroup, transfer to a department in which you would rank higher on the seniority list.

- *Join the untouchables.* There is another reason to seek other departments. Reductions in force rarely occur evenly across every department. Some departments can be hit hard, while others are not even touched. Transfer to one of the untouched departments. How can you identify a safe department? Look for one that has been doing a lot of recent hiring. These people know they are safe and certainly received corporate's approval to expand before doing so. Do you see a lot of new faces? Join them.
- *Demonstrate superior morale.* Subconsciously—or maybe even blatantly—your boss wants to get rid of morale problems. She might not have the ammunition to do it in normal circumstances, but a mass layoff gives her the needed opportunity. Keep your job by being the model of a positive attitude. Stop short of cheerleading, but make it clear that you like your company, enjoy your job, and love your boss.

Dealing with Job Loss

OK, you have done your best, but one day your boss's assistant sticks her head in your office and advises you to "go out and check what you thought was your parking spot." Whether it is caused by a layoff or an individual selection, there are some things to do immediately after receiving the news.

First, Do Absolutely Nothing

Resist the temptation to call business associates or contact search firms within the first few days. You haven't had a chance to develop a plan for your job search, and you will scare off people who could be helpful later on. Further, you will undoubtedly be bitter, angry, or, at the very least, certainly not your best. You do not want to be talking to a potential employer until you have adjusted your attitude.

Deal with Your Emotions . . .

If you are not upset at losing your job, then you are in denial. Job loss has a tremendous emotional impact, ranking right up there with divorce or death in the family. You must deal with the grief, or you will not be able to move forward productively. A common example of this is someone who has unresolved resentment toward the boss who fired him. This bottled-up anger comes through in a job interview; the job seeker comes across as hostile and difficult to manage.

Don't think you can hide your emotions. Job loss is a violent shock, and it generates powerful negative feelings. Refusing to deal with self-pity, anger, or failure may make a potential employer think you are aggressive or nervous. Continuing to feel embarrassed about losing your job will keep you from appearing self-assured and confident.

. . . As Well as Your Family's

The frustration and fear that you feel during this crisis are minor compared with what your family is experiencing. While you go through these exercises to give you comfort about your finances and potential job opportunities, your family is probably hearing nothing but silence from you. Understand the terror this creates when they know about only the crisis and not the opportunities.

Keep your family informed. Let them know exactly what your financial situation is, your plans for dealing with job loss, and opportunities that may be knocking. Also, describe your real fears, and explain the negative impact that this will have on their lives. These realities—both the positives and the negatives—will reassure them and help them deal with this family crisis. (How can detailing the negatives reassure them? Because if you do not explain the bad things that will happen, they will imagine far worse things. Just like you, they will grossly exaggerate the consequences of job loss.)

Keep your family informed. Let them know exactly what your financial situation is, your plans for dealing with job loss, and opportunities that may be knocking.

I have seen too many families in unnecessary pain—even torn apart—because the person experiencing job loss thinks it best to go it alone. Involve your spouse and children in every aspect of this crisis, and watch your family grow stronger as you face this struggle together.

Survey Your Situation

Job loss is indeed a crisis, but most people overstate its impact. Take stock of your situation and explore your options. Analyze your financial situation. How much time do you really have to find another job? By following some of the suggestions made later in this chapter, you will see that you are in much better shape than you immediately thought. This analysis will bring you tremendous emotional relief as you realize that you do have the time to deal with the crisis properly.

Let's look at some aspects of this financial planning and see how to organize yourself in dealing with this life crisis.

The Severance Package

Long ago, clans that wanted to get rid of their workers without killing them would instead burn their houses down. Thus the term, *getting fired.* Things have improved a bit. There is a good chance you will see some sort of severance package instead of seeing your house burn to the ground. Unless you have a contract that provides for it, there is no legal requirement for your employer to provide severance pay.

Here are the typical components of a severance package:

Money. Most companies provide severance pay to help ease the pain as you seek new employment. Companies may pay this in a lump sum or simply have you remain on the payroll for a certain amount of time. How long? It varies radically. Lower-level workers may receive two weeks' pay. I have seen packages for midlevel executives that extended a year. (I had an ex-boss who was simultaneously drawing three severance salaries from previous employers while in his first year as senior executive of a fourth. These results are not typical.) When dealing with large layoffs, companies often use an arbitrary formula, such as a month's salary for each year of employment.

> A man is not finished when he is defeated. He is finished when he quits.
>
> —Richard Nixon

Outplacement. At the time, you will consider salary as the most important feature of a severance package. But for the long-term impact, outplacement assistance with a solid, professional outplacement firm is your most valuable piece of the package. Push hard to have this included in any package you may be able to negotiate. Professional outplacement firms will help you structure your job search, deal with your emotions, and get you to work faster. In addition, you're with others who are going through the same thing, and you can develop a great network.

Medical insurance. Under the Consolidated Omnibus Budget Reconciliation Act (COBRA), companies must allow employees to keep their health insurance coverage for eighteen months after they leave the organization. This means you can maintain the coverage you had during employment. However, you must pay for it, and it's usually a lot more than you expect. This is because you have to also pay the company's portion, plus an additional fee of up to 5 percent.

Vacation pay. I mention this because accrued vacation pay is not a severance gift; it is your right. Just like salary that has been earned but not yet paid, accrued vacation is something that is owed to you. While the laws on this vary from state to state, the moral principle is universal. Do not let the company deny you this money upon any termination.

> I never thought that I didn't have a card to play.
>
> —*Apollo 13* Commander Jim Lovell

Bridging to retirement. Class companies will grant time for bridging to retirement if an employee is within a few years of eligibility. This is usually in the form of adding years to age and service with the company. It costs the company little if the organization's pension plan is funded. Thus, if the company does not offer it initially, it is a good item to negotiate for.

Stock options. You usually have ninety days after termination to exercise vested stock options before they are lost. Most people are scared to spend cash during a period of unemployment, so these valuable assets may be jeopardized. You should negotiate to extend this period.

Negotiate Your Package

You have more leverage than you think during these times. Companies doing layoffs are quite sensitive to their public image and want to maintain the image of fairness if at all possible. And most companies want to do all they reasonably can to accommodate people being laid off; this has a strong effect on surviving employees and future recruiting efforts. (I once sold a candidate on going to work for a company based on the fact that it had a history of providing exceptional severance packages.)

> Companies are most flexible when faced with feeling they are being unfair during these times. Do not hesitate to push this button.

Go to your employer with your requests if you do not feel the package you're being offered is reasonable. It may not be able to accommodate all of your requests, but you may be surprised with its flexibility. For instance, do you have special needs? If circumstances make it hard for you to find work or imperative that you not be without steady income or health coverage—perhaps your spouse or child has a serious illness—appeal to the highest levels of management in writing. Companies planning a large layoff usually budget for unforeseen expenses. Senior management can use these funds to address your special situations.

Also note that you can often ask for extras that cost the company little or nothing. For instance, you may be able to maintain an office for a few months or retain your phone for receiving messages. Extended use of the company car may be reasonable, especially if you offer to pay for its maintenance. You have a good chance of having your request accepted if the benefit costs the company little yet has a big impact on you.

Companies are most flexible when faced with feeling they are being unfair during these times. They are sensitive to being criticized for being mean during terminations. Do not hesitate to push this button. When faced with a separation package, look for something that makes your situation different from the typical worker's. Analyze how you may be treated unfairly in this process, and focus on these needs.

Financial Planning

There are two reasons for getting a grip on your personal financial situation. The first is obvious; you need to budget wisely right now. But the second reason may be more important. You need to release the panic that naturally occurs when first faced with this crisis.

This process will put your situation in its true perspective. For instance, while you initially thought the world was crashing in and your family would be soon living on the streets, seeing that you actually have several months' resources can provide enormous comfort. You will be thinking from a rational perspective instead of an emotionally charged one. Obviously, your decision-making abilities will improve dramatically.

> He's no failure. He's not dead yet.
>
> —William Lloyd George

Finding a new job may take some time, and you will need to maximize your ability to deal with it financially. If you are forced into a quick job search, you will be tempted to pursue situations that could spell long-term career disaster. Here are some suggestions for maximizing your options:

- *Prioritize your debts.* The first entries on this list fall into the must-pay-without-fail category. These include mortgage, car, utilities, and health insurance payments. You must have a place to live and a car to go job hunting.

- *Make sure you have health insurance.* You cannot risk racking up massive debt through unexpected medical emergencies. If your spouse is working, you may be able to join his or her plan. If that's not an option, then you should sign up for the COBRA coverage we previously discussed. COBRA is expensive, but the alternative could be life shattering. If you drop your coverage and become ill while you're out of work, you may not be able to get insurance in the future. And if you or someone in your family requires major medical care while you're uninsured, the costs could bankrupt you.
- *Make paying the mortgage and utility bills a top priority.* If you fall behind on your mortgage, you could face late fees or even the loss of your home. Even if you will have no trouble meeting your mortgage payments, call your mortgage company and let an officer know your situation. He has faced this before and will often have programs to offer to help you, especially if yours is an FHA loan.
- *Call creditors.* Credit-card debt may seem like a high priority simply because the creditors are the ones who scream the loudest for payment. While you certainly want to maintain good credit, these debts should go to the bottom of your list. However, call your creditors and let them know the situation. You'll actually find them understanding and helpful—if you are the one to initiate the call. Your situation is not uncommon to creditors, and they have several programs they can pull off the shelf to help.
- *Defer student loans.* The Department of Education has deferral programs. It will even pay, in some situations, the interest during the deferral period. Call loan administrators for details.

- *Maximize your income.* File for unemployment insurance. And do not let pride stop you. Your employer has been paying into this fund for this very reason. It is not a government handout; it is your money. Sure, a couple of hundred bucks a week will not replace your income, but it will certainly extend your ability to cope with the crisis. Is your spouse working? If so, change your tax withholding. You'll probably fall into a lower tax bracket, so it is unlikely you will end up owing the IRS. Also, your spouse may want to temporarily discontinue 401(k) contributions, which will increase take-home pay.

> If life was fair, Elvis would be alive and all the impersonators would be dead.
>
> —Johnny Carson

- *Avoid meddling with retirement accounts.* While you may choose to temporarily suspend retirement plan contributions, do not take money out of these accounts. You'll have to pay taxes on money taken out, plus a 10 percent early-withdrawal penalty.
- *Consider taking a part-time job to bring in extra cash.* Please note that I am emphasizing a part-time situation only. The cash is needed, but it is more important that you have ample time to conduct a solid job search. For your long-term career health, the job search must have priority over any income you may derive from working full-time instead of part-time. I understand the pressure and temptation, but trust me on this one.

Public relations consultant Ralph Reed adds this perspective on shaping your own "Bounce Back."

Make your own path. Don't become a victim of conventional wisdom in your career and calling. Be creative; use your talents and skills in whatever way you feel led.

Think of recent presidents. Ronald Reagan was a radio personality, a film actor, and a union president—one of the most unusual paths to the presidency in history. George W. Bush is the first MBA to ever sit in the Oval Office, a former energy executive, and a baseball executive—again, a highly unusual path to the presidency, but he followed his loves, his interests, and his talents. There is no one way to serve others. Each of us is unique, and our careers reflect that God-given uniqueness.

Think of the trapeze artist as you build your career and consider new opportunities. A trapeze artist always lets go of one rung before the other reaches him. For a split second—that can seem like an eternity—the artist hangs in the air exposed to great danger.

That is what a career and life can be like. Making changes and leaping at opportunity is not without risk. Indeed, there is a great correlation between the amount of risk and the amount of reward. I spend a good bit of my time encouraging successful, capable, and happy people to risk all they have to enter public service and seek elective office. There is great risk in this endeavor—financial, personal, and professional. But the gain to serve others is huge.

There is no way to grab that trapeze without letting go of what you already have—no matter how comfortable or safe it is. *Sometimes you have to jump before the trapeze is there.*

Employment Options

Some employment options become available to you when you are laid off that are not as readily available when you are looking for a job while still employed. Yes, you actually do have some advantages over the employed. Consider these targets:

Competitors. They would love to have access to your experience and hope they also learn some inside information. If you are in sales or have contacts with potential accounts, competitors will generally show you the red carpet.

> Remember, even monkeys fall out of trees.
>
> —Korean proverb

Vendors. You have probably developed a good relationship with people and companies you have been buying from. Vendors usually know of other companies that might be a good fit. (They hope that you will remember their help and become an even more loyal customer at your next company.) Their introductions can often be as powerful as an inside referral.

Customers. In many cases, your customer base might be an excellent source of employment or referrals. Again, you have already established a relationship with them. Their familiarity with you and the work you do reduces the risk in hiring you. Do not hesitate to approach customers and let them know of your job search. Most will respond enthusiastically.

Board members. Large layoffs trouble most board members. Although they are probably removed a bit from the details of the layoff, they are familiar enough with the circumstances to have an interest in the employees affected. Most of these board members are associated with other companies. While they wouldn't dream of approaching people employed by your company, they will often be positive toward hiring you now.

Franchisees. You have a tremendous resource if your company has franchisees. Many of these franchise companies are just miniature versions of the company that just laid you off. Their needs usually include the services you provided the franchisor.

Get ahead of the crowd and immediately contact every franchisee in your organization. (Are there some that you can't work for? Contact them anyway—they will provide incredible referrals and references.)

Overqualified: Another Way to Say Age Discrimination?

What is most on your mind right now is looking for a new job. We covered the bulk of this subject in Chapter 11, but I do want to focus on one subject that seems to be a plague on job seekers who have been downsized. So many of the jobs you will apply for are a notch or two below your previous level. Sometimes you will be rejected for those jobs with just about the silliest term I've ever encountered. They'll say you are *overqualified.*

The overqualified hurdle is a tricky one. While it's nice the employer recognizes your value, it still leaves you scrambling for a new job. Recognize that there are two categories of people who get labeled this way:

1. People who have been unemployed for a long time and are desperate to take any job. Employers know that these people will quit just as soon as something better comes along.

2. People who are genuinely looking for a career or life change.

> Failure is an opportunity to begin again more intelligently.
>
> —Henry Ford

Your job, of course, is to convince the company that you are in category two, not category one. This is easier to do if you are genuinely in category two and not actually desperate for work.

Employers are worried that you misunderstand what the job entails and that you will reject them once you are presented with the details. Employers hate to be rejected, so they reject you first. You can offset this concern by simply knowing what the job is all about when you apply for it and showing genuine interest during the interview. There must be some aspects of the job that present new challenges and opportunities for growth. Make note of them and emphasize them during your interview.

Before you try to change hiring managers' minds, take their concerns seriously. Evaluate the potential job, compare it to your situation and goals, and decide whether these fears are legitimate. Will the type of work hold your interest? Would you treat coworkers as peers? Is a lower salary going to satisfy you? If you can persuade *yourself* that you are a good fit for this position, then try these strategies to persuade the potential employer.

Get in the door. If the employer tells you over the phone that you're overqualified, see if you can get an in-person interview anyway. A face-to-face meeting presents many more opportunities for bonding as well as the opportunity to address concerns directly.

Exude flexibility. Help the employer see you in a new role by showing you can adjust to the company's needs. Stress your ability to adapt to the company's needs and priorities. Give examples of how you have done what was needed to get the job done, regardless of rank or ego. Point to places on your résumé where you have worn many hats.

> It isn't over until I win!
>
> —Les Brown

Emphasize skills, not titles. Highlight the kind of work you do rather than the specific titles you've held. Change the language in your résumé to focus on skills. If the stated requirements for the position are a subset of your skills and experience, then tailor your résumé and cover letter with experience that matched the requirements—and not a single word more.

Don't scare the boss. You will often interview for a job a notch or two below your previous one. That often means that you are sharper and more qualified than your potential boss. He will be paranoid enough about this possibility on his own. If you present yourself as a potential threat, he will eliminate you just to preserve his own job. Try not to come off as someone attempting a hostile takeover. A little modesty pays. If you offer suggestions for improvement, also mention some areas where the company shines. Also demonstrate your capacity to take direction. Talk about a successful relationship with a previous boss or professor.

If all else fails, be direct. Ask them, "What can I do to convince you that I'm the best person for the job?"

Demonstrate commitment. The company thinks you'll quit just as soon as a better position presents itself. You can counter that fear by pointing out your longevity in previous jobs. Explain that you are willing to take a step down because of your interest in working for this particular company or industry.

Grab them by the throat. If all else fails, be direct. Ask them, "What can I do to convince you that I'm the best person for the job?" Also, ask your interviewers to describe the ideal candidate. Then, point by point, show them how your qualifications match this description.

And Finally, Keep Notes

Pay careful attention to how people respond to you while you are down. Some will disassociate themselves from you because you are no longer useful to them. It will hurt to realize that these people were close to you only because they thought they could get something from you. Even though it's painful, acknowledge the fact.

On the other hand, you will be rewarded with learning that

most people will draw even closer to you. These people were supporters when you were on top and may even show greater support when you are down. Accept this friendship and revel in the deep riches it represents. (Refer to the closing scene of *It's a Wonderful Life.*)

> Failure is God's way of saying, "Excuse me, you're moving in the wrong direction."
>
> —Oprah Winfrey

The fact is that *you will bounce back.* It might be a short time or it might take a couple of years, but good people always land on their feet again. In the near future you will be at or above the position you were in before your fall.

And here is a gift that your downfall will have given you: when you return to the top, you will have a very real evaluation of the people who surround you. You will know for a fact who your friends are, how strong your family is, and who can be counted on. Looking back, you might even eventually conclude that your down period was a good thing for your career in the long term because of this perspective it provided.

Although his beloved Britain rejected him in 1945, Winston Churchill was not at the end of his career. The very next year he made his "Iron Curtain" speech, which became the basis of foreign policy for the free world. He was returned to power in 1951, where he again led his nation during the difficult early years of the Cold War. After retiring in 1955, Churchill wrote a six-volume history of World War II and won a Pulitzer Prize. He lived out his life as an elder statesman and contributed his incredible wisdom until his death in 1965.

Winston Churchill was not an average person and certainly

did not live an average life. His successes were of grand proportion—and so were his failures. And he refused to allow this defeat to be the end of his story, just a redirection leading him to even more successes.

You will have failures along the way. Some of them may be devastating and painful. But failures are not the end of your journey. They are lessons to be learned and opportunities for new things. You will discover that these challenges make you stronger, smarter, and better focused.

You will recognize that Winston Churchill's wife was right.

CODA

One Saturday afternoon, the firefighters at Station 8 were gathered around the table, enjoying one of those legendary dinners that firehouses are so famous for. As the bowl of cheese jambalaya was passed around for third helpings, the conversation morphed into a dreamy discussion of how their lives would change if they won the $200 million lotto to be drawn that night. There were the usual discussions of mountainside homes, luxury cars, and even owning a pro sports team. Talk of jewelry, unlimited golf, and European vacations filled the air. Jeff was unusually quiet during the discussion. "You know," he said, "I really don't think the money would change a thing about my life." Before the jeers of his brethren reached a crescendo, he added, "Except maybe I would buy me a tub of rocky road ice cream and eat the whole thing by myself."

No one in the group won the lotto that evening. But three days later, after their dinner of spaghetti and giant meatballs, the group called their partner aside and presented him with a half-gallon of rocky road ice cream and a spoon. They had collected five bucks and made Jeff—at least by his definition—a very rich man.

So, what is success, anyway? What is it that we are all chasing? There is wisdom in the old saying, "Life is a journey, not a destination." People nod their heads when hearing this, but how many believe it in their hearts? When asked the question "Are you a success?" there can be but two possible answers: "Yes" or "Not yet." As long as you treat it as a journey, the answer can never be no.

Let me share the most important thing I learned in the process of writing this book for you: The greatest career crisis is *not* failing to reach your career goal. The fact is, you almost certainly will attain your career goal. No, the greatest tragedy actually occurs when you fight, sacrifice, and sweat your entire life, reach the mountaintop, and then realize it was the wrong mountain. The single biggest factor in achieving career success is picking the goal that is right for you.

Successful people are those who know what they really want and understand what is important to them. Once people know what they want, they usually have little trouble getting it. It is a bit humbling to recognize that this huge personal discovery could have been made just by paying attention to Curly in the movie *City Slickers*, when he declared that the secret of life is "one thing."

You can have anything you want. You just can't have everything you want. Know what you want, and you will achieve it.

Let me close by sharing with you some great insight on the definition of success. George H. W. Bush was being interviewed, and the interviewer tossed a softball. The interviewer listed Bush's accomplishments: war hero, successful businessman, ambassador to China, director of the CIA, UN ambassador, vice president, president, father of a president . . . an incredible list. Then he asked, "What are you most proud of?"

President Bush replied, "The fact that our children still come home."

I hope this book will help you set your career direction, grow in your job, and respond to changes and challenges. But most of all, I hope I've been able to help you keep your career in perspective. Discover the purpose God has blessed you with, put your family first, treat everyone with respect, and follow peace in your decision making.

And never, *never*, order barbecue in Maine.

ABOUT THE AUTHOR

Ken Tanner began his career scrubbing dishes in a Pizza Hut and eventually became the youngest manager in that chain's history. What followed was a twenty-year career in the hospitality industry. He served as regional vice president, director of training, and COO of companies such as Taco Bell, Long John Silver's, and Advantage. This phase of his career featured dramatic customer-service turnarounds, record-low employee turnover, and the development of dozens of leaders in the industry. He is especially proud of the number of women he helped advance into executive positions.

At 37, Ken retired from the restaurant industry and founded an HR consulting firm. Initially focusing on recruiting, Ken now uses his expertise to help companies build teamwork and retain employees as well. Companies of all sizes—from small family-owned enterprises to Fortune 500 corporations—have benefited from his workshops, culture surveys, recruiting services, and consulting.

Ken's passion for developing people has led to his founding of *Solomon's Harvest*, a program that matches, trains, and supports mentoring teams. He and his family live in Marietta, GA, where he also leads the *Mayberry Family Bible Study*, a popular summer class at Johnson Ferry Baptist Church.

Ken Tanner is available for seminars and speaking engagements.
He invites your contact at kentanner@consultant.com or visit
his Web site, www.kentanner.net.